Janet,
Some giggles!
Enjoy!
Bill

…just saying!

Observations and opinions of an old salt

William Stephen Dial

Without the coaxing and coaching of *my adult leadership* this compilation of columns would not have been possible. Thank you Susie.

Contents

Forward

That's Sean and Clancy. They're good boys.

For many years I wrote a column for a now defunct newspaper. I called them conversational essays. I wrote about the kinds of stuff one might discuss sitting at a Tiki Bar somewhere on the edge of the great Chesapeake Bay. Most were humorous…some a little serious. My wife, whom you will discover was called *My Adult Leadership* in my pieces, has suggested more than a few times that when I had nothing else to write about, she and the dogs became the foils.

For years I surveyed boats. For those of you who might not know of this trade, I inspected boats for sellers and potential buyers seeking to properly value the boats and identify things that might not be proper…or were really nice. Great job until the recession of 2008 and my ageing bones suggested I should play in another park. In the course of my surveying years I met some very delightful and interesting people. And I wrote about them and their boats…and, on occasion, their plight.

I grew up in a time that now seems to be forgotten in an area of the world that could be the stand-in for the Garden of Eden, the *Panhandle of Florida.* It was paradise and I've written about it.

I hope you enjoy my observations and opinions...I'm just saying.

Aesthetic Obsessive: *I finally realize I've lost control*

I knew it was just a matter of time. I just didn't realize how quickly my time would come. Now I've lost control. I should have realized. My first indication was a trip to Annapolis, Maryland. It seemed innocent enough. A simple request to go shopping: *To pick up a few things.* I needed a few things too. I was feeling pretty good. After all, I had the boat I had been wanting: real man's boat; big CAT diesel; a work boat; a wooden boat. But it was the boat that was the beginning of the end.

It started with the bimini, that umbrella like apparatus that covers the cockpit of the boat, and the boat's canvas: the wrong color. In my obviously deluded opinion, the bimini and canvas were a beautiful burgundy. The boat was predominantly gray. What could be wrong with that? *Well,* I was told, *that's because you're a winter. Of course you would like the darker colors.* If you're confused, it's okay. I'll help you. God knows I wish somebody had helped me. I had to go it alone. You see I'm married to a person with an aesthetic obsessive personality. The shrinks don't have a code for that yet…they should.

This winter thing has to do with one's colors. No, not your school colors...the colors God gave you at birth. I have kind of a ruddy complexion, ergo I'm a winter. You can be any of the seasons. I don't remember what my wife is—vernal equinox or something. Anyway, she's a strawberry blonde which means any color that I like she thinks would better suit an undertaker. There's a book about this. Helps you decide what season you are so you can choose the right colors. Aesthetic obsessives know about these things and it guides their lives.

I thought it was kind of cute when we started dating. I had this great sweatshirt. I paid extra for it because it was guaranteed not to shrink. I hate it when sweatshirts shrink. But the sweatshirt was yellow. That's okay by me. I like yellow. Nope—wouldn't do. Winters can't wear yellow. Turns out whatever season she is has yellow right at the top of the hit parade. Lost that damn sweatshirt by the third date. And then she hit my closet. My madras sport coat? Gone! That coat was a babe magnet. Stepson though—has her coloring—could wear all my stuff she rejected. Should have been a clue.

When we met, I lived in an apartment in a house I owned. I had remodeled the whole thing to suit me. I had planned to move aboard a boat and use the apartment as sort of a place to go when the boat was laid up. It had nice greens and burgundies and blues. Manly colors. She was subtle…at first. I could see my decorating scheme didn't exactly float her boat but she didn't criticize. I had my various trophies and things arrayed here and there. My dog seemed to like the place. She, the dog, never complained.

When we got married, the logical thing was to move in with her. I had no problem with that. My *live-aboard* plans were long since sunk. I figured there was someplace in a house occupied by a wife and two stepdaughters that I could claim as my own; a place to set out my old Viet Cong canteen and my miscellaneous car parts. There was a place—the attic. The three women just couldn't see the beauty in an old double hose SCUBA regulator or a greasy chain tensioner from a Porsche 911. Somehow I lost every vote.

Now I'm not hard over. That house was one pretty place. Some of the rooms were a bit shocking—I'd never seen bright coral walls before. There were creams and yellows and pastel thises and thats—no hunter green or burgundy anywhere. The flowers were exquisitely arranged, the beds and curtains all matched. I didn't even know you could do that. I'd never heard of Laura Ashley. Molly, my sweet black lab didn't seem to mind even though she is a winter like me. She was trying to make friends with the snarly blond cocker spaniel who already lived there. Anyway, I was blinded by love. I could adapt.

Well, the years passed. The aesthetic obsessive adapted a little too. In my navy days when I wore khaki uniforms she didn't complain, even though winters are not supposed to wear khaki. I learned, in matters aesthetic, to keep my mouth shut. I eked out a little cubby in the smallest bedroom—put out my books and my treasures; hung a *no girls allowed* sign on the door (Molly can't read). I found solace in my few things and the girls knew better than to mess with anything in my lair. Sure did get dusty in there but it was my dust.

We moved to the Eastern Shore of Maryland. I painted where I was told to paint and with whatever color I was provided. House looked like one of those house-tour places but that's okay, I planned to get a boat: my boat, a real man's boat. Boat like that I could decorate in a manly way.

Finally, my boat came in. I thought it would suffice to name it after her. No, it's not the *Aesthetic Obsessive*, though that crossed my mind. It's a sweet name for a sweet lady. At least she was sweet before she started decorating my damn boat. Which brings us back to the trip to Annapolis.

In Annapolis they have everything you could ever want for a boat. I had a few things in mind. I needed a new radio. Thought I might get a storm anchor. Thought I would look around and see if anything else tickled my fancy. I had not planned to go to the Nancy Hammond store. Who's Nancy Hammond? Ask your wife. Nancy Hammond paints wonderful scenes from The Chesapeake Bay. She paints dogs and sailboats and scenes that anyone who loves The Bay can truly enjoy. She has a store near the Statehouse. Well, my boat now looks like an annex to that store. I have dogs and sailboats and scenes from The Bay all over the inside of the cabin, each piece carefully chosen for its predominant colors. Give me a break. I knew curtains were next.

Well, I want her to enjoy the boat too so I can bend a little for the interior of the cabin but last weekend she went too far. I got that radio I needed. I had some free time so I thought I would install it in the boat. The boss was out arranging flowers or something…improving the aesthetics of the world a little bit at a time. I sort of gave up on my ideas for the cabin. But the bridge, that's my space. I've got some good ideas for making that perfect. And the engine…well, you can't improve on CAT yellow.

I put the radio up above my head, over the window. My hearing is a little deficient…rode in too many helicopters: having the radio right above my head might help I thought. Half way through the job, guess who wanders down the pier? Yep. I should have just packed up and gone home. I should have known there was no way that radio could be in the right place. *Why there?* she sweetly asked. That question is a little like when the cop asks if you know how fast you were going. There ain't no right answer.

Well, we tried it here and over there and over beyond the GPS and it still belonged over my head over the window. I held out. You would be proud. By the time we had discussed all the places that were more aesthetically pleasing, it was too late to finish the installation. I'd have to wait until next weekend to finish. I ain't no dummy, don't think I believed she had given up. I'm pretty sure she was perfecting her arguments. I held out. That radio was not going the way of my Madras sport coat. My radio. But I knew the end of this struggle was not ended. I realized I had lost control. I just didn't want her to suggest painting the boat a *warm coral.*

Cooter Catastrophe: *I almost died because of a turtle*

Did I tell you about the time my grandfather almost killed me? I didn't? Well, it started with a cooter, Southern for aquatic turtle. This cooter was not a cute little terrapin: it was a big, ugly alligator snapping turtle. I mean double ugly. Ugly as week old road kill. With a personality like my first mother-in-law before her morning coffee. I grew up around these monsters and I learned early on don't mess with them. They're mean. I know, somebody's going to get their knickers in a bunch and defend these critters but you might as well save your time. One almost got me killed.

On occasion, in the Northwest Florida swamps where my family fished, turtles would be caught. It was custom to kill the turtles, the theory being that they were, in part, the reason nobody ever caught any fish. On one occasion, in a part of the swamp called Moccasin Slough, grandfather caught an alligator snapping turtle. We were fishing from an old wooden jon boat cobbled together from pine with a seat almost all the way forward, a live well with a hinged seat on top in the middle and a seat aft. These were very functional craft but were not *purty* as we said in the South. I'm telling you this because the boat plays an important role in this tale.

When grandfather snagged the turtle he uttered some words never heard in church. I'd guess that turtle weighed twenty pounds, maybe more. Grandfather hauled the beast aboard continuing his soliloquy of doom for the poor reptile. The poor reptile was not impressed. In fact it was some put out. For a few moments the turtle just rested there in the bottom of the boat clacking his beak, probably considering its best line of attack. In these pre-disaster moments, grandfather, still cussing, was digging his fishing knife out of his tackle box and contemplating herpetological decapitation. Then, as they say, the sierra hit the fan. Turtle made his move.

The alligator snapping turtle has a pronounced beak. His uppers look parrot-like. From my vantage point at the forward end of the boat it was clear to me that that turtle had no intention of allowing grandfather anywhere near it with a knife. Indeed, that turtle had vengeance on its mind. Alligator snapping turtles look big and clumsy with short, little, scaly legs and a big domed carapace. Do not be fooled…turtles can move out if the situation requires. In its armor plated mind, that turtle sensed requirement. Grandfather could also move fast if required. He grabbed the boat's paddle to fend off the turtle. All old wooden jon boats had a wooden paddle. The paddle was usually scraped from a pine plank with a draw knife…crude but functional. Alligator snapping turtles have been known to bite clear through the handle of a paddle like that. The turtle sank its beak into the blade of the paddle. It did not like having an eight-foot long paddle stuck on its beak. It ripped that paddle out of grandfather's hand and started swinging it back and forth, windshield wiper fashion. Grandfather, sensing he was about to be pummeled, stood up on the back seat of the boat and did some kind of Celtic fandango to avoid the swishing paddle handle. This is when grandfather decided to shoot the turtle.

Up until then the scene had been rather amusing. The stream of invective directed towards a turtle was pretty funny all by itself. Watching grandfather dancing on the stern seat avoiding the swinging paddle was downright comedic. Up until then there wasn't much I could do to help…I wasn't getting anywhere near that turtle. Then grandfather managed to get his snake-gun out of his tackle box. I could tell right away things were going south.

Almost everyone who fished back in my day had a snake gun. Rattlesnakes and moccasins were ubiquitous. Snake guns were usually the cheap little twenty-twos the police called *Saturday-night-specials*. Grandfather's was of that ilk and rusted. That gun might be little but it can still hurt. Grandfather was doing the Riverdance on the back seat while trying to get a bead on the snapper. I was considering a swim.

Well, he did it. Kapow. That little bullet didn't stand a chance against that armor plated reptile. I heard the ricocheted bullet zing by my ear. I was starting to abandon ship when I realized the gun was jammed. It was so rusty the cylinder didn't turn. About then the turtle managed to bite through the paddle and realizing it was in the company of a madman, lumbered overboard. Having recovered from getting nearly shot I started laughing, you might say hysterically.

Grandfather, at this point, allowed as how I should have saved him from the vicious turtle and I suggested it was he who wanted to slit the poor critter's throat and might be considered vicious himself. We pulled up the cement-in-a-juice can anchor and headed back. I was sworn to secrecy and told I would never get to go fishing with grandfather if I ever told. I didn't…tell or go fishing again with grandfather.

A Bunch of Old Geesers: *I go to a lodge meeting with a gaggle of old geesers*

My friend Hogan called the other day and invited me to his lodge meeting. Hogan, you probably recall, is the yard boss at the Itty Bitty Boatyard of the Eastern Shore and is an Eastern Shore native: 3 generations and Methodist. I have known good old Hogan more years than either of us wants to mention and I never knew him to be a lodge man. And I told him so. Hogan tends to get a bit testy when he thinks you're doubt'n him: he let loose with both barrels, *You don't know everything about me. My lodge has been dormant because of the moratorium on goose hunting. I belong to a goose-hunting lodge. And I thought you might be interested in meeting some fellow geesers but I'm about to change my mind. Calm down*, I said, *I'd be proud to meet some of your lodge buddies. What's the name of this lodge? It's the local Gaggle of GROG,* he said, *The Greatly Respected Order of Geesers. Oh*, I replied.

Hogan picked me up in his old pickup, the one that looked like it had been brush painted with cheap boat bottom paint and smelled like a crab house dumpster. On the seat next to Hogan was what appeared to be an ancient Inca chief's headdress. *What's with the feathered fedora?* I asked him. *You really are dumb aren't you?* he snapped. *This is a goose hat. If you bothered to look, you'd see that it's as handsome as any gander that every crapped in a cornfield.* Alright, I replied, *how come you're so defensive? I'm not defensive. My wife warn't too nice about that hat either.* I was beginning to understand.

Hogan told me that this was a serious lodge and I had better behave or I could find some other boatyard to mooch coffee from. I can take a hint so I stopped smirking. We arrived at a country store that belonged to a mutual friend and retired to the back room. Hogan warned me that I was considered a *gosling* and I had to take an oath not to reveal the workings or plans of the lodge. I put my left hand on a book of Department of Natural Resources hunting rules and raised my right hand but before I could repeat the oath, some new arriver came up behind Hogan and goosed him. That's what they do instead of the secret handshake. Well, Hogan jumped so high he forgot the oath so I feel like I can share these things with you.

As I looked around the room, I was powerfully amazed…every darned one of them had on a hat that looked like the head of a giant goose. And they were flopping around in what resembled black swim fins. I sat as far back in the room as I could.

The Grand Gander honked the meeting to order with a beautiful, cherry wood, goose call. I understood much of what he was saying because I've read all about hunting geese in magazines. Some of it was a little alien though. I learned that a pair of singles was really just a pair of geese flying without the rest of the skein, they're only a gaggle when on the ground. I leaned over and asked Hogan why they don't just say a pair of geese. He gave me that look again and I shut up.

The next speaker addressed the upcoming lodge fundraiser. He said they couldn't serve the goose fritters like they planned. Seems they had lots of goose meat but it came from resident golf-course geese. Resident geese all taste like cigar butts, which make up a big part of the resident goose's diet. I'd never thought of that.

An old man, who looked like he was older than my first mother-in-law's bad attitude, stood up and was recognized by the Grand Gander with a double honk on the goose call. This gentleman must have been something really special in the brotherhood because he had the hat and a set of gray wings. He started his talk with a few comments on the decline of the sport of goose hunting and how much better it was in the days of the *punt gun*, an oversized shotgun, when one blast could take out a couple of dozen geese. He really was an old geeser. His next topic was the Gaggle's new goose pit, a hunting blind.

The new goose pit was obviously very special. From my seat in the back, the architectural renderings looked pretty impressive. At first I thought it looked like a subterranean blockhouse…like you'd find on a missile range or something. Then I got to see a blowup. Amazing! It was on a creek off the Choptank River in Dorchester County Maryland, whose location was known only to full-fledged members of the Gaggle…which left me out. The pit wasn't a pit in the traditional sense, it was reinforced concrete and lit and heated by a Caterpillar generator that could power a small town. The generator had the *quiet package* usually available only to the military. Would you believe a periscope? Yep, just like a submarine. You could raise it up and look all around. Speaker said you could see a ruffled feather on a goose a hundred yards away. What really impressed me though was the hydraulic shooting platform. If geese were spotted commingling with the decoys, the shooters whose turn it was stepped from the heated room into a closet-like thing and were raised to shooting height by a hydraulic lift. Amazing. And the dogs had a little heated room too. When they came back all wet and dripping, a current of warm air dried them and made them ready for the next trip. The geese they retrieved were dropped into a bin that was kept chilled to right temperature. The whole thing was *bushed-out,* camouflaged, with fiberglass phragmites, reeds, so you don't have to go out there every year and replace them, an onerous chore. That darn goose pit had a big-screen TV too.

When the old geeser got to the new decoys with the remote control system like the ones that guide the unmanned spy planes over Afghanistan, I was ready to believe most anything. I wouldn't have been amazed if he had next talked about some kind of laser designator sight system that *painted* a goose in the air so you could take him out like they take out an enemy plane with an anti-aircraft missile. I thought I had heard it all.

When the meeting ended I was still in shock. Hogan said I had done okay and hadn't embarrassed him too much. I said I appreciated his inviting me and had enjoyed meeting his friends. I allowed as how I probably wouldn't apply for membership though. I don't hunt anymore. And I would probably break some essential bone walking around in those black swim fins.

The Galloping Wudjas: *I reveal Christmas just wears me out*

I've been run over by a herd of wudjas and I'm flatter than a possum on a freeway: worn out, pancaked, nothing left. Around Christmas the wudjas possess certain folks like cheap-movie aliens, turning ordinarily nice people into monsters. The wudjas tend to herd and stampede and anybody in the way is done for. At first you don't notice them, wudja do this, wudja do that: sort of innocent. Then they start to run and heaven help whoever is in the way. The wudjas possess my adult leadership at Christmas and I barely the stomping.

I'm sort of indifferent about all the hoopla at Christmas. I'd be perfectly happy just thinking about peace on earth and goodwill towards everyone. I guess I don't have many fond memories of Christmas growing up. But my adult leadership lives for Christmas. She's already planning next Christmas and this year's season is barely over. I'm not an old Christmas grouch like that green critter up on the mountain; I just don't get overly excited. But the boss does and long ago I promised myself that I would do everything I could to make her Christmas bright. I'm an idiot.

I'm big on peace. I think that's what Christmas is all about, right? So I try to maximize my peace...a good book, a pot of coffee, a little quiet. Wrong! I think the decibel level in our household goes up to about 100 right after Thanksgiving and stays that way until well after January first. Why it's necessary to turn the freaking Christmas music up to maximum is beyond me. Johnny Mathis sounds just as good, maybe even better, without blowing out the stereo speakers. I can no longer handle Handel: hallelujahs at 100 decibels make me decidedly un-hallelujah-like. I like the word cacophony: jarring, discordant, sound. Christmas is cacophonous at our house. *Wudja turn that volume back up, Mannheim Steamroller is about to do Rudolf.* Get the picture? Steamroller indeed. Every time I settled on the couch, a stream of wudjas attacked.

The absolute worst wudja is the Wal-Mart wudja. *Wudja run to Wal-Mart and pick up* [something or other]*?* I think Wal-Mart is a great store. Thousands of others think Wal-Mart is a great store too...and they are all there at Christmas. Wal-Mart people usually have the nicest smiles. Not at Christmas. Snarley only begins to describe their grimaced faces. Mind you, I'm not criticizing. I'd be snarley too if I was being overrun by dozens of faucet-nosed, ankle-biters and their exhausted mothers. Wal-Mart's so crowded around Christmas you have to park in the next county. Pack a lunch if you're going to Wal-Mart at Christmas because getting to the store from your parking place is nothing short of a hike.

Another wudja that irks me is the *do me a favor* wudja. I know I'm not going to like that one the moment it comes at me. When the perpetrator throws out that favor-clause, it means some chore that is so nasty guilt has to be employed to get it done. Why else would *a favor* be imposed? I mean, just a plain old wudja might possibly offer a little bit of an out, after all, the root word in wudja is *would* which implies an option. I am, however, no fool. A normal wudja is not fraught with options: a *do me a favor* wudja offers none.

Another guilt-steeped wudja is the *hold the grandchild* wudja. I love my grandchildren. They are all sweet, never smelly and always polite and they don't throw food. But I don't like holding babies. I feel like I'm holding a grenade, the pin of which has been pulled. Most of the time, they don't like me holding them. That's why they start to scream the moment their grandmother deposits them on my lap. I think the respective grandchildren-parents have observed this *deposit-scream* phenomenon and seldom go through the drill...but not grandma. I think she thinks the noise of a child screaming adds color to the background noise of somebody's church choir electronically decking somebody's halls yet again: see cacophony above.

I do most of the cooking in our house. I like to cook. When I'm in the kitchen, I'm at peace. I don't like to share the kitchen when I'm cooking. It has to do with people interrupting my peace. Around Christmas my kitchen is full of people interrupting my peace. *Wudja just be nice* is one of the wudjas I hear regularly. I'm not being *not nice*: it's all those people in my kitchen who are not being nice. It's my kitchen. People bumping into me, raiding my cabinets, purloining components of whatever I'm cooking, asking me questions: sheese! A person could be excused for being a little grouchy.

Why is it my adult leadership does not understand that keeping our social calendar is her responsibility? I'm not alone in this: guys back me up. I have plenty of things I have to worry about. When we're going to somebody's house for cocktails or dinner is not one of them. So when I say, *What are we doing tonight?* and the response is *Wudja try to keep track of what we're doing?* the answer is no. I don't have to. My adult leadership keeps lists. I trust her lists. Why would I need to keep lists when she's already keeping lists? Similarly, why do I need to keep track of what we're doing when I know she's already doing it? Makes sense to me. Somehow, the adult leadership finds humor in the fact that I don't keep track. She giggles when she tells all her lady friends that I never know what we're doing. They giggle too…so I really don't think I'm alone in this.

Well, another Christmas has come and gone. I did all the wudjas I could. I didn't get much peace but everybody seems happy and that matters. Next year I'm going to disappear right after Thanksgiving and not be heard from until Easter: I think that'll finally get me some peace. All those little wudjas will starve to death and that's a good thing…keeps them from breeding. In the meantime, I'll lick my wounds, have nightmares about Wal-Mart shopping during Christmas, and try to get over being stomped by the galloping wudjas.

Boat Shoe Demography: *footwear tells a lot about people*

Boat shoes are responsible for the stupidest thing I ever did. My former wife wore boat shoes. She was okay to look at to be sure, but that wasn't what got my attention. She wore a pair of beat up boat shoes to a study group one Saturday morning. We were supposed to be working on problems for a graduate marketing class but all I could do was look at that girl in the boat shoes. Later on in the morning I asked her if the shoes were an affectation or was she really into boating: said the shoes were for real. I was smitten. And stupid.

The premise was good though. In the old days people in boat shoes were likely to be kindred spirits. You could only buy boat shoes at boat stores. To be sure there were things called moccasins that sort of looked like boat shoes but they weren't. Leon's, what the cognoscenti used to call L.L. Bean's, didn't even sell boat shoes until the late 70's. You had to go to the boat store to get boat shoes; ergo, if you were wearing boat shoes you probably knew something about boats. Saw somebody in boat shoes you could strike up a conversation, *You a boat person? Wanna get married?*

There were only 3 types of boat shoes back then: 2 eyelet, 4 eyelet, and those soft ones made out of something like beige elk hide. You could tell the kind of person by the type of boat shoes they wore. I fancied myself a two-eyeleter. Two eyelet boaters drank wine from screw top jugs. Light beer was when the long neck bottle was half empty. Suntanned women who wore khaki shorts and wore two-eyelet boat shoes were where it was. The boats, power and sail, were fast. You didn't see any of those smarmy little stainless steel grills either. After all day on the water, you spent the evening with food cooked over the embers of a beach fire. Socks were forbidden and we owned a lot of madras.

The 4 eyelet types were the *G and T* bunch. Sort of snobby actually. I guess they needed the extra arch support the additional 2 eyelets provided: wallets were probably heavy. This group owned big sailboats with sniffy New England names like Dreadnaught and Valiant and Challenger. A few had powerboats: always big old displacement hull cruisers and motoryachts. This group could actually spell burgee and knew whence to fly them. Four-eyeleters attended lots of committee meetings and had houses on or near the sea. Blazers were big with the 4 eyelet crowd but they were more likely to be worn with Breton red slacks or the lime green ones with the little blue whales. Socks were optional with this bunch.

And then there's the beige shoe crowd. They were something else. Actually, they were too few to be called a crowd. This group was fond of titles: Commodore this and Colonel that. Single malt straight up if you please. Their boats were usually overlarge sailboats always manufactured in Bristol, Rhode Island or someplace else in New England inaccessible without a pilot. The few powerboats in the group were heavily varnished and often driven by a poor masochist who called himself *professional captain*. This bunch wore blazers with the little embroidered pocket doohickeys that advertised to the world that their yacht club had dues equal to the domestic product of more than a few small countries. No option on the socks.

When my former wife introduced me to her proper New England family, her mother whispered, *He's not one of us*. She had undoubtedly seen my 2-eyelets and arrived at a quick conclusion. I'm sure she explained to her daughter, my fiancée, that this was bound to happen when she started slumming…wearing those 2-eyelet boat shoes. I'm fairly certain she admonished that her family had always been 4-eyelets and her dad was nearing the beige boat shoe level. I was doomed. I was 2-eyelets forever. The rest is history.

Times have certainly changed. I've seen blue boat shoes, sandal boat shoes, and boat shoes that look like my old *PF Flyers*. I've seen boat shoes on people whom I know have never even seen a boat. What is to become of us?

I think my premise though has not changed. I started a little unofficial survey from the vantage point of a nice stool at a local Tiki Bar. You can still tell a lot about somebody by the type of boat shoes they wear. I'll exclude from my survey the fashion conscious types who wear boat shoes because they think it's cool but wouldn't get near a boat. That crowd is beneath contempt.

The PF Flyers gaggle wears socks. Really, they wear socks with their boat shoes. That's the *muscle shirt* bunch: big gut, gorilla hair and ugly shorts. This group always has the babe in the bikini close at hand. She never wears boat shoes: usually has on a thong…sandal. PF Flyers always arrives in a boat you heard fifteen minutes before he got there. Boat has flames painted on the sides: often has flames coming from the engine compartment.

Now the sandal boat shoe crowd, they're left over from the sixties. Usually have classic sailboats or kayaks. They meditate a lot. As a friend of mine says, *They like to get naked and drink green tea*. There is an exception to this category: the cerebral crowd. They drink green tea too but stay clothed. The thinkers would rather analyze the effect of wind currents on their sail's center of effort than actually sail.

Bridge club ladies wear the blue boat shoes. They don't handle dock lines, these ladies. Mostly they ride in trawlers. Sometimes they harangue the *professional captain* for sport. They're big on arranging the flowers at the yacht club. They still wear pleated skirts. Back when they were undergraduates, they wore 2-eyelets but that's a family secret.

I guess us Boomers have to get used to the proposition that nothing is eternal. The stylizing of boat shoes had to happen I guess. After all, us boaters are pretty cool. Emulating our fashions was something we should have expected. Me? I gave up on my 2-eyelets. Had to go to something with more arch support. Buy my boat shoes at the outlets now. I never thought I'd wear boat shoes with soles of any color other than white but the shoebox declares that the brown soles are non-marking. The ones I wear have this little *high fashion* kiltie thing on them. They're pretty comfortable. No eyelets though. That would have confused the hell out of my former mother-in-law.

Aholics Anomalous: *I eschew aholics-ism except maybe...*

I've got a friend who describes himself as a *Pop-Tart aholic*. Addicted to the things, he is. We're not talking the babe with the ventilated knickers type of pop tart here; we're talking Pop-Tarts of the toaster kind. I asked why he doesn't just smear some Smuckers on a saltine, a confection infinitely more desirable to me. Not the same, I'm told. I'm obviously lacking. True Pop-Tart aficionados are cult-like: they slink about the aisles of grocery stores snatching packages off the shelves and squealing like they've discovered some rare and exotic vintage. They can explain nuances like normal people would describe nice wines: truly addicted. Really weird!

I got to thinking about this *aholics* suffix that we see appended to so many things these days. I love neologisms and am not beyond inventing a word or an appendage to a word when I think the normal offerings do not suffice. I have a few favorites and they pop up in my columns occasionally. But the *aholics* thing has gained broad acceptance and is used to describe some strange addictions.

I have another friend who describes himself as a *NASCAR- aholic*. Now that's one for the *aholic*-record books. Their numbers are in the tens of thousands. Used to be we'd say we were fans of something. But the term fan is pabulum. It just doesn't describe in sufficient depth the true feelings of the true *aholic*. Fanatic is probably a bit over the top: fanatic connotes some wild-eyed misanthrope, slobbering and sloganing. An *aholic* probably has not yet achieved fanatic but is nipping at its heels. My NASCAR friend is very close: he has the shirts, the bumper stickers, the sippy cup. He drives down the road making stock car noises with his teeth: pathetic.

There's another group which I include in the societal anomaly, the *aholic*. That's the sports-*aholic*s. I'm not going to spend much time here. You know them. I know them. They have little decals of the cartoon kid whizzing on their team's most hated opponent: tell me that's not in the margins of society. Actually, I'm kind of envious of this group. I sometimes think I'm a little weird (Hush!) because I've never been that enthusiastic about something. But they are a little strange. I can't help but giggle when I see a grown man walking around in what looks like satin bloomers patterned after his favorite team's livery.

The suffix *ophile* used to be accepted and even respected. I'm a *bibliophile*. I love books. Sadly, that suffix took on a sour note when it was hijacked by the psychiatric industry to describe persons skewed way, way out on the margins. One dare not say one is an *ophile* anymore for fear of someone hearing only part of the term. Book *aholic* just doesn't seem to work: sounds like an addiction to the lottery.

This brings to mind a serious question of the use of the subject suffix. I'm talking dedicated chess players: a chess *enthusiast* works but doesn't quite go where you want to go. *Chessophile* sounds like some overlarge reptile seen snorkeling near the Thomas Point Light in the Chesapeake Bay. Chess-*aholic* definitely doesn't work. Google both those terms and you get big bunches of hits so I'd say chess players, as a group, have an identity problem. I'm proposing, *Chesster*: One who is an enthusiastic chess player. Mr. Dillon would be proud.

Now, everyone knows where *aholic* came from. In the original term it was oholic but suffix thieves are known to be a scurrilous lot and not only purloined the suffix, they unabashedly altered it from its original form to cover their tracks. The etymologists call *aholic* a pseudo-suffix. That's okay with me: they can call it anything. It has gained acceptance in the language and everyone knows what it means. It's just that you see it applied to so many strange things.

What on earth is a scrapbook-*aholic*? When you see *aholic*, you envision one who is so besotted they cannot be out of contact with whatever their addiction is. Now, apropos scrapbooks, that presents some interesting images. I see a person sleeping with scissors, glue, shreds of pictures of Aunt Minnie and those cute dogs, and all the other accouterment that accompanies scrapbooking. I did see the term scrapbook-*aholic* used so it's authentic. I couldn't make something like that up. I have to admit that I've seen scrapbooking bumper stickers so maybe the level of enthusiasm exceeds my appreciation; however, I've not seen the tee-shirts yet so I'm suspicious. Scrapbookers, you need to whip up more excitement (see cult above). (Late note: eBay has Scrapbook-*aholic* tee-shirts.)

Now, after having said all this about *aholics*, I have a confession to make. My name is Bill and I'm a Reese's Peanut Buttercup-*aholic*. No, I don't sleep with peanut butter cups but I've been known to hide them in secret caches. Those little peanut butter ball things you see around Christmas…those too. I know, I said I wasn't addicted to anything but here's ample evidence. I've given it some thought; I'm joining a twelve-step program a soon as I can find one addressing my particular anomaly. I'm not alone in this…comforting…my stepdaughter shares my addiction. I guess we can confess to each other if we can't find a group.

My beloved adult leadership, now there's an *aholic*. I wasn't supposed to say this but I've already read this to her so she won't know. Coffee Ice Cream: that's her addiction. Disgusting: talk about being on the margin. A few years ago an ice cream parlor opened in the village of Oxford, Maryland where we live. The Scottish Highland Creamery makes ice cream unlike any you've had before: always a queue on weekends. Victor, the ice-creamologist, and a bona fide Scot, and his lovely wife Susan, have tapped a sensitivity. I suspect my adult leadership may not be the only addict suffering in the queue. I observe the line at the Highland Creamery strictly as an interesting study in sociology. You see, I'm above this: I refuse to succumb. Normally staid citizens literally stand there blurry-eye with little rivulets of drool oozing form the corners of their mouths, the discussion focused on the made-fresh-daily offerings in mango, Mexican vanilla and other frozen fantasies. Every strata is represented: NASCAR- *aholic*s give up their zoom-zoom, the scrapbookers lay aside their scissors, no one is playing chess on the picnic table where patrons sit not caring that their butts are glued to the tabletop by the dribbles of those that have gone before. My wife gets a far-away look as she devours a double scoop in a waffle cone. I'm so proud of myself for not joining this spectacle: except when they have peanut butter and fudge; I cannot resist, I am not a man of steel.

Spelunking in the Chittlins: *I forego all dignity*

I feel that it is necessary to share with you an onerous healthcare experience. It was a humbling experience. My adult leadership, being of the feminine gland, does not understand the humiliation a man feels when he undergoes this particular procedure and has enjoined me to proceed with caution on the off chance that others of her gender might read this. I've promised.

First, I believe in colonoscopies. I really do. They are intended to check for signs of colon cancer, a disease that claims, unnecessarily, many, many lives every year. And I've had several…colonoscopies. Necessary though they are, there is no way you can get beyond what must be done before, during and after that invasion one's most secret places.

It's funny how the medical profession approaches matters as delicate as having your chittlins checked. You get this piece of paper in the mail that tells you what to do. The instructions remind me of what my father used to say…fairly often, *This is not going to be nice but it's for your own good.* Well, that first part is right: nice it ain't. The instructions are terse, totally absent of anything that might be used in a court-of-law if the colonoscope gets a short circuit, hits a pocket of gas, turns your innards into strawberry jam and blows the roof off the procedures room. They tell you what your diet should be and about the special stuff you have to buy to *prep* yourself: to the point, professional. But there's something missing. Oh yeah! There is nothing that says indignity is inherent in this procedure but they know, they really do. You can read between the lines. They don't care. And you can see from what they tell you that this means humiliation and they know you know they'll be laughing, all of them. They can't wait until you're lying there exposed and dozens of people are standing around pointing to things and commenting that they're amazed you ever fathered children and, not only that.... . Well, you see what I mean. And when you whine just a little your other half says you're a wuss. But you have to follow the instructions: can't have those pockets of methane.

This prep business is worthy of a little discussion. There is nothing on the face of this earth that can make a clear diet palatable. Those instructions seem to imply this is something people do every day. Go to a restaurant and say, *I'll have the clear diet special.* And they bring you out a steaming bowl of dishwater. I haven't eaten, and I use that participle cautiously, Jell-O in years. Now I remember why. And broth...has to be clear. I bought two kinds, both produced by a company of national significance. Both tasted like bilge water. Anybody who packages stuff that tastes like that should be suspended by their thumbs...or better, forced to undergo a colonoscopy with a fire hose.

But the diet's not the worst part, no sir. The worst part is that stuff they make you drink and the consequences thereof. Oh yeah, that's a thrill. Two little bottles, each an ounce and a half. I've seen what a stick of dynamite can do. I've seen avalanches. I've been exposed to hurricanes. Nothing, absolutely nothing, has the power of those three ounces. The stuff tastes like lime flavored brine. You add it to a little water, choke it down, and then grab on to something solid. Gut wrenching, pile driving, earthquake rumbling, quickstep inducing, never get more than 3 feet from the throne, powerful. That stuff will make you hate the day you were born. By the time you're done, you'll feel like you've been eating jalapenos for a month. The mere thought of anybody approaching those parts causes cold sweats. You've seen those pictures of the baboons with the red butts? Get the picture?

Then the day arrives. You have to bring someone with you to take you home because they're going to put you in la-la land. That's a relief because you need to be anesthetized before anybody gets near the inflammation. Of course you have to wait. This is, after all, a medical procedure and to not wait would make you suspicious. And of course your innards still sound like an Amish buggy on a cobblestone road. And, of course, you have to use their rest room and all the soothing, lotion impregnated tissue is at home (see *inflammation* above). Muffled screams can be heard throughout the building.

Finally the nurse comes and gets you. You hug your wife and make sure she knows where all the legal documents are and that you don't want your children to get your firearms because of the grandkids. They take you to a cell with a curtain on the door that's seen too many trips in the dryer, big gaps on both sides. They hand you a gown that's ridden the same number of trips in the dryer. The nice nurse lady smiles and instructs you to strip to your socks. I wasn't wearing socks. The breeze felt good on the inflammation.

They plug in the IV so they can get the happy-juice in faster and the doc comes by to encourage you. *Let's see, only a half-dozen polyps last time. You shouldn't have nearly that many this round.* Made me feel better. I woke up in the middle of the last one and saw the inside of my insides on the TV screen. Some device that looked like Pac-Man was nipping at the wall of my colon and little trickles of blood were flowing down. Went back to sleep and dreamed that my first mother-in-law was operating a little tiny backhoe.

The joy juice goes in. The doctor asks some profound question and that's the last you remember.

Later you wake up back in your cell and your wife tells you've been there for a half hour. She says the doctor came by and you told him a dirty joke and you drank 3 glasses of orange juice and you don't remember a thing. Your gut feels like somebody used you for a balloon and you're starving. Wife says the doctor only found one of the little devils and it appears benign. Best news is you don't have to go through this again for about 6 years. Yippee!

My chittlins are slowing recovering. That balloon feeling went away…suddenly…an hour or so after arriving home. I'm glad I had the procedure. I've slowly recovered use of my…well, the inflammation is nearly gone. There is comfort in knowing that I don't have any signs of colon cancer. That alone makes the whole ordeal worth it. If you haven't had a colonoscopy, you're a wuss.

Good Bye Good Friend: *I deal with a great loss*

It was one of the saddest moments of my life. One has few opportunities to bond the way we did. In both sleep and awake we had been together. Friends. Soulmates. I had many times been cradled in its arms. On those miserable nights when I was troubled by myriad things, I could find comfort with it. I didn't want separation: I got loss. It is too painful to even ponder. It was the best damn nap sofa ever made. And my wife gave it away.

That sofa and I had been friends for many years. I remember when it arrived. I had been away. It replaced a wicker contraption that creaked when you sat on it and left horrible impressions on your head if you happened to doze off. I did not regret its disappearance. But the new one...I saw immediate possibilities. It was striped with blue and yellow: not unattractive. The upholstery was a comfortable denim-like cloth. When it comes to aesthetics I've been told I have developmental problems...so I've learned to keep my opinions with regards to the appearance of things to myself. But I liked this new sofa right away. Remembering the pain one experienced with the wicker thing, I was, at first, quite tentative: I feared disappointment. I had learned that comfort always plays second fiddle to beauty in our house. Then, with courage not unlike that of the great adventurers, I settled into its upholstered depths.

One thing I don't understand about the species we call mother is why they feel compelled to continue this mothering behavior in the extreme, even after their progeny are old enough to fend for themselves. All of our children are grown. All have jobs which very likely exceed the pittance I bring in as a pensioner. So why does my wife think she needs to furnish their houses? And the poor kids: maybe they don't want a striped sofa. I mean, they are still hung up on those futon things. Talk about uncomfortable. I always ask if that's what you put your futon where does the rest of your body go. They don't seem to think that's funny either.

I have seen lots of things go out our door that I thought still had a little life. I think the kids take them because they don't want to hurt their mother's feelings. I have noticed on our visits things they have been given appear in odd places, like maybe they were retrieved from the back of the closet just so they wouldn't bruise their mother's sensitivities. I've tried to tell her: maybe you should let them decorate their own houses. Maybe they don't like taupe and coral and striped sofas.

I've got this little table. Attractive little thing. It has four or five *tv-trays* that slide in and out. You just pull one out when you need it, the rest of the time it's a pretty table. Now that's a practical piece of furniture. I got it from the credit card company during one of those promotion things. These are not flimsy trays: they are substantial and of good wood. It has served as an end-table and served well. Sometimes it's nice to have a little tray to put things on when you're sitting on the sofa. When it was just my black lab Molly and me, we put popcorn and beer on those little trays. Molly liked popcorn and beer. Then we got married and we were told our little table of trays was passé. I don't think Molly ever quite recovered from that slight. I have managed, to date, to hang on to it but I think its days are numbered. You see, we're redecorating the family room.

I came home from work recently and the family room walls had a half-dozen different colors of brown paint on them. Remember what I said about being aesthetically disadvantaged: I knew I was in trouble. The room had been a cheerful yellow. I'm reminded often by my adult leadership that at first I didn't like the yellow either. Actually, I didn't like it when it was in the can: it looked different when applied to the walls. We had yellow walls and the trim was a pretty white. There were blue accents and my beloved

43

sofa was blue and yellow. I was happy. People from all over commented on how pretty the room was. Then something happened.

I don't know who or what caused the spasm that resulted in a need to redo our family room. The sofa was a little faded and had this tiny little hole in the upholstery. Nothing, I thought, serious enough to warrant its removal. Next thing I know there are upholstery swatches and those little paint thingies that have the different colors on them positioned all around the family room. Women do that periodically. I think it's sunspots or maybe excessively high tides that cause it. Usually these things pass and everything goes back to normal. Then the little tiny paint cans appear. The decorating places are on to women. They sell little cans of paint that cover about a square foot. That way you can test the color on the walls. That's how come the walls of my family room look like the wreck of a painter's truck. Well, I started to get nervous. None of this stuff seemed to match my sofa. Then I was dragged to the big city. I should have been suspicious when somebody made a doctor's appointment for me…to get my eyes checked. That way, I would have dilated pupils and not be able to comment on anything. Uh-huh! I'm so naïve.

After the doctor finished and I was totally blind I got led to somebody or other's fabric store where I had to look at this beautiful sofa that I couldn't possible see…my pupils being the size of quarters. This, coupled with my known lack of aesthetic sense and my good sense not to comment on the aesthetics of anything, did me in. Next thing I know I had agreed to a new sofa and my nap sofa was doomed to relocation to a kid's house.

Well, after a fashion word came that the new sofa was soon to arrive. I helped the kids load my nap sofa into the back of their truck, trying hard to suppress my tears. I cannot tell you how sad that moment was. My beautiful nap sofa, maybe a little faded, maybe a little tattered, disappearing into the back of a truck. I got out my folding chair that I bought at WalMart for ten-bucks, you know the kind that fits in its own sock, and set it up in the family room: wasn't pretty but at least it's mine. The void where my sofa had been gave me this creepy feeling: someday, when I'm a bit tattered and threadbare, I might be shoved into the back of some truck to be hauled off to a place where I'll get no respect. I made some popcorn and opened a beer and pulled out one of my little trays.

It arrived. It is pretty. Seems to be comfortable but a little shorter than my nap sofa. I can probably make do. Needs a lot of breaking in. So far I'm told I can't put my head against the cushion unless I put a dish towel behind my head…don't want to dirty the thing up. And the new ottoman… no feet on that please. We had to buy a new blanket to drape the thing in so my dogs can climb up and cuddle in the evening…they never had to do that with my nap sofa. I think it hurts their feelings. I have this comfortable chair up in the bedroom…it's not allowed in the family room, doesn't fit. But it is a fantastic nap chair. Think I'll just go upstairs.

Words: *I have fun with malapropism*

I went to see my friend Hogan the other day. Hogan runs a little marina here on the Eastern Shore of Maryland. His family's been on the Shore for a long time and he calls himself a native…and almost everyone else an interloper. I'm his friend to be sure but I know where not to go with Hogan. When Hogan starts to talk politics, it's time for me to drain my coffee cup and hit the road. The other day I couldn't escape.

Apropos of nothing we had been talking about, Hogan grumped, *these politicians beat the cake. Do what,* I said, stifling a grin. *You know what I mean,* he snarled. *They're just beating a dead horse to death.* I assumed he meant the politicians, the subjects of his ire, were continuing to focus on an issue Hogan believed had been resolved. I really wasn't sure. I was so tickled by his choice of expression that I was not focusing on the thesis of his comments.

I love malaprops, named for Mrs. Malaprop, a character in an 18th century play by Richard Sheridan. Malaprops are usually words or clichés that someone messes up. My friend Hogan is a notorious malaprop. My first wife was one also often declaring that, *Misery is its own reward.* Ain't that great? I miss her. I worked with a guy that, on his best days, was a horse's butt. He was always talking of something that would *exasperate* the situation. Of course he meant *exacerbate*: to make worse.

Pompous people seem to be the guiltiest of this sort of thing. They strut around and pontificate and try to make you believe they have something nobody else has. Then they open their mouths and you realize the jerk's all bluster. One of these people with whom I was acquainted claimed to be an *aficiocondo* of good wine. He certainly wasn't an aficionado of good English.

Misuse of words and phrases though is not just the province of idiots. I had a friend, gone now, who had at least a dozen fractured phrases he regularly employed. One of his best was when he declared something had become a *flaw in the ointment*. Another was *dead men spoil the broth*. In the middle of a very serious conversation, he would let go with one of these and I would have to contain myself. He was a very bright and considerably educated man.

I remember that President George Bush was known to use creative clichés and the occasional wrong word. Some folks think this is a sign of ignorance or inadequate education: not me. I think it's the sign of someone who is trying too hard. If I had all the people sniping at me that a sitting

President does, I suspect I would screw up a word or phrase periodically too. After all, *to err is human and that's divine* as my first wife would say. President Bush, I believe, is a real person, not a pompous phony. Makes you want to say, *A Bush in the White House is better than the birds at hand.*

I've always marveled at the elasticity of our language. New words and phrases, or at least carefully crafted variants of old familiar words and phrases are always showing up. I think that's a wonderful thing. There is nothing stuffy about American English: need a word and can't find it, make one up, most of the time no one will know the difference.

During the reign of my former spouse we were separated a bit for the convenience of the government. I went overseas and she went off to school. We were reunited after about six months. In those six months a new expression had gained a foothold at home. She kept using the expression *big time*, describing a major occurrence. I had not heard these words used in that manner. An informal survey of my friends and colleagues revealed that they had not heard such as well. Before long though, everyone was using the expression *big time*. I think sometimes expressions sort of creep up on us. We hear words on television or the radio and they become part of our vocabulary without our realizing it. This, I believe, is *a good thing*. I have to admit though that I plan to strangle the next person *big league* that I hear using the expression, *at the end of the day.*

Not that many years ago I had my first computer class…well; maybe it was a while ago. I was exposed to bits and bytes and hard drives and a world of jargon that was akin to a foreign language. My classmates, for the better part, had about the same level of competence in this field as I. Today we take computer words for granted. Today, the average 6 year-old is fully proficient in computer jargon. One wonders what new language is in the offing. I think maybe it will have to do with *nanotechnology*: Learning that will be no small thing.

My friend Hogan fancies himself to be very politically savvy. He studies all the positions and generously provides his commentary. I love to hear him get all worked up when he disagrees with something. I think if I were to describe his approach to politics the word Ninja would arise. After watching and hearing him go on about the physical abuse he would like to apply to several of the most recent candidates, I thought it best to be on my way. I didn't want him to confuse me with a politician. As I left, he yelled at me, *I'm tired of people treating these politicians with golden gloves.* I'm not sure he fractured that.

Garden Grief: *My adult leadership confounds me*

I think, maybe, just maybe, I've planted the last danged thing in the garden this year. I can't be sure about that. Her horticultural majesty is very fickle about these things. We have now exceeded the garden budget times about three but that is not why I believe I'm done. I'm done because I've had it. I mean it. Absolutely done. Unless, of course, she finds some other something that the garden will not survive without.

I believe here in Oxford, Maryland, where we live, gardening comes a close second to boating. Some might argue that its number one. Whatever. I just know behind and, in some cases, in front of every house is a garden. And they're pretty too: lots of flowers, green bushy things, purple bushy things, and scads of exotic whatzits. And everybody walks around and comments on everybody else's garden. Even have a tour so that you can see who's caught up on their weeding and who hasn't deadheaded the damn delphinium or whatever.

You got a garden, you got no privacy either. Seems you put in a garden it's like an open invitation. I'm sitting on the john with the door open so I can keep the dogs from eating the cat's food and three little old ladies go by the window headed for the garden. You got a garden, you got no privacy.

My momma was a farmer's daughter. When she was still able she liked to grow things. We had the prettiest flowers in the world. We had beds and beds of colorful things. She didn't know much about English gardens or feng shui—more on that later—or anything else except what tasted good and what was pretty. Momma, I'm sorry I ever complained about shelling peas or weeding the garden or any of that stuff. Those were such simple times. Those were such beautiful gardens.

Now, for those of you who don't know about feng shui—I pronounce it *fung shooy* to just let her horticultural majesty know how I feel about these things—it is something the ancient Chinese came up with when they got bored building that wall. Give you a little background: lady here in Oxford had a touch of conflict with the boatyard across the street. She put a little bitty mirror on her fence to bounce the *ill will* back at the boatyard. I wanted to tell her she needed a much bigger mirror. I know some of the folks in that boatyard. But that was the feng shui thing to do. Harmony and balance…it's all about harmony and balance. I was told my dresser was out of balance, had to rearrange its top. I never thought my dresser was out of balance. Never fell over. I was called a cretin.

After I complained about my dresser, her majesty decided we needed a professional feng shui consultation. She commissioned the mirror lady to give the place a once over. Knowing about that mirror, I wasn't too optimistic. After she was done, I was amazed we had done as well as we had for so long. I had to move every picture in the house. I had to put money in corners. Plants had to be thrown out. New ones had to be moved in. I drew the line when I found out my ragged old jeans weren't feng shui.

So once the house got feng shuied, the ladies took aim at the garden. I was beginning to like that garden. I had worked hard digging holes and planting things. I tested the soil and I augmented it and it was starting to look real pretty. I complained a little bit. I allowed as how I thought it needed some four-o'clocks and some gladiolas and, maybe, a few of those lilies like my grandmother had growing out by the chicken yard. I was called a cretin. But then, along came *fung shooy*. All those things I planted had to be moved. Out of balance! What? Yep, had to have the marriage corner and the money corner and I nearly needed the coroner. Turns out colored flowers are not harmonious. Purple and green bushes—that's harmony. Then she went after my fruit trees. I've only got two, a peach and an apple. And the squirrels get all the fruit anyway. But those are my trees. Inharmonious indeed. I won that one but not before I had to prune them back to seedlings.

And then there's that urn. Now I live in a waterman's town. Only urns around here used to be out at the cemetery. Not anymore. I got this concrete thing with lions' heads on it. Fellow sneaks out back to relieve himself cause somebody's in the loo, is likely to start a twelve-step program when he sees those lions. But they are, by-gosh, harmonious.

When I went through my *I'm done planting* routine the other day, her highness snickered. You remember that hole you dug out there the other side of the lion urn? We've *got to get the perfect tree for that place. One more trip.* I caved. We went to Davidsonville, west of Annapolis, to the garden store-llama ranch to get the ultimate, fung shooy bush. I knew I was in trouble when the llamas scared hell out of my dogs. My boy-dog was so unnerved by those ugly things he hid behind his momma for gosh sakes…I told her we shouldn't have had his hoo-hoos snipped. Took several cookies to calm him down. I left him trembling in the car while we went looking for that bush. Well, we found it.

Of course this ultimate bush had to be something oriental, feng shui and all that. I don't know why, in this time of patriotism and American awareness, we couldn't get an American tree, nice oak or something. Not even; it had to be a Japanese Maple. All this buildup I had received, I expected to see something with some substance, the kind of tree one of those shogun warriors would be proud to pause behind. It's going to be in the marriage corner...should be strong and sturdy like a good relationship. This piddly little thing won't last past the first nor'easter blows through here. Wouldn't know it by the price though. That little bush cost three boat payments. And it was one-sided. What happened to balance? It was missing all the limbs on one side. I was called a cretin.

Well, that's it. I'm not going back to the garden store ever again. I've had it. And one of these nights, when I go out back and if the lions don't get me, that fung shooy bush could be in real trouble. I didn't think those llamas looked all that safe either. Cretin indeed.

Clown College: *I, at least, feel better having said it*

I love old P. T. Barnum. P. T. was up front: the real thing. He was the founder of the circus that became Ringling Brothers and Barnum and Bailey. He is famous for the quote: *You can fool some of the people all of the time; you can fool all of the people some of the time, but you can never fool all of the people all of the time.* Some folks say Abraham Lincoln might have said this too but P. T. usually gets the credit. Whether it was P. T. or Abe, it matters not: they represent both of the schools about which I'm writing. P. T. was a circus man, Abe a politician. I've decided politics and the circus have much in common: they are comprised of clowns.

P. T. was famous for his sideshows. He had the 3 rings to be sure: the high wire, the trapeze, the pretty ladies, the clowns. But he was really famous for the sideshows. He fooled multitudes. He relieved lots of people of their hard-earned jingle in those little tents leading up to the Big Top. As you worked your way towards the giant tent, the barkers shouted descriptions of the spectacles inside their smaller ones. Old P. T. was not beyond *phonying-up* something and selling it to the folks as the real thing. That's sort of what's going on American politics too: a bit of *phonying-*

up. It seems to me that politics has become little more than spectacle, its substance has about as much veracity as old Barnum's sideshows. And it really doesn't matter which Party is doing the barkering; they're all trying to fool us.

As a kid, I remember going with my father to political rallies. They were great fun because there were other kids there and who wanted to listen to an adult standing behind a podium shouting like a revival preacher. Not only that, there was always fried mullet and coleslaw and all that sweet iced tea. Sometimes there was banana pudding. But my father took these rallies very seriously. And after a candidate spoke, he…or she…answered questions. And I recall my father discussing with my mother some of the positions taken. Often he questioned the verisimilitude of a candidate. If something didn't ring true, the candidate was requested to explain…in front of a crowd that, on occasion, could get downright rowdy. Many years later I discovered that much of what was said in those rallies was untrue. There was a political machine in the county where I grew up and successful political candidates were little cogs, mere teeth on much larger wheels.

On one occasion, by happenstance, my father witnessed a figurative political assassination. A Congressman had fallen from grace because of personal avarice, his activities threatening the machine. My father was on a business trip and was invited by an associate to the conclave where this Congressman's future was decided. The meeting was held in a dark, smoky shack on the banks of a large North Florida river. Bankers and politicians, other bigwigs and poor folk alike gathered around a table normally used for butchering game, sipped moonshine and good bourbon, and made decisions with serious national implications. The Congressman wisely chose to pursue other opportunities.

It seems to me that the information age has produced national level machines. Gone are the days of smoky fishing shacks and smoked filled rooms. Today a candidate gets vetted not by the positions he or she truly espouses but by convoluted metrics, which defy simple description. When was the last time you saw a truly physically ugly national level candidate? I know some really smart, really ugly people. Do you believe for a moment that this shallow metric would be ignored when selecting a national level candidate…or for that matter at any other level? How often do you hear, following a debate or interview, commentary on the candidate's appearance? Often more is said about this factor than any other. The machine *don't want no ugly cogs*.

And talking points: in the comfort of your television room you never see *talking points*. You sure as hell hear them though. Has it ever struck you as curious how six or eight talking heads will use the same phrases? That's because they got the fax and you didn't. The big machine wants to make sure the product has zero defects. Years ago I was the legislative assistant to an important person. Hated the job. Had to take three showers every day to get the political stink off. My person was true, straight as an arrow. But his positions, whether he agreed with them or not, had to reflect the positions of the politicians appointed over him. It mattered not that my boss's positions could have meant whether some mother's child lived or died: it had to match the talking points. And we got them every day. Got them by fax from friends on the hill. And on the 6 o'clock news I saw talking heads spouting with faux profundity every dot on the left of the page. And they looked right in the camera and recited just as though those positions came from their very souls. Gag me with a spoon.

In some ways I'm a phony. I claim no interest in politics. I avoid discussing politics with my friends. But deep down, I'm my father's son. With interest that begins in my very being I watch the candidates. I listen to the ads. I watch the debates. I listen to my friends discussing candidates. All this while eschewing politics…at least by appearance. Lately I feel more and more like I'm being taken for granted. I have some strong feelings about some national issues. I don't think either party is adequately addressing my concerns. I think there are many who share my positions but don't have the marbles to stand firm. I know the argument: a politician who commits political suicide in a campaign will not be very effective later. But we've let them get that way. We don't demand that they explain to us their intentions. We just listen to ad after ad where they batter their opponents and don't say squat about their own plans. They just pitch those talking points. That's what the national committees have said will sell…polls and focus groups have said so.

I wish I could draw cartoons. I would like to draw a clown car. I would open the doors and have dozens of politicians spilling out dressed in all the clown stuff. If I could do this, I would make sure you could identify the faces of the politicians. You and me, we have created a clown college. We elect these people and they go to the capitals/capitols and do little more than entertain us with their antics. P. T. Barnum would hire the lot. They flop around in their clown shoes; their squirting petunias pinned to their lapels and they make us laugh. And they laugh too. You can't be a clown if you don't enjoy the job. We laugh at them. They laugh at us. It's a lot of fun being a clown. Us spectators, we paid admission. Now we get entertained. And they've got sideshows too. Over and over we hear the barkers shout: *Step right up folks, we've got social security and healthcare and national defense. Come right in and let us show you these monsters.* You'll be entertained.

Another thing P. T. Barnum said that I like: *You'll never go broke underestimating the intelligence of the American people.* I wish it weren't so.

Hot Dog Demographics: *Once more I try to figure folks out*

From time-to-time I have explored upon these pages those characteristics I believe define us as citizens of this great nation. I have delved into the intricacies of one's choice in boat shoes and arrived at some conclusions that I believe rival those of Freud and Jung with regard to typing personalities. Similarly, I explored choices in boats as a method of categorizing personality. I believe the Myers-Briggs folks are examining my findings re boats since they pose a threat to the near universal Myers-Briggs personality-typing (I'm an INTJ). Today I'm announcing…right here…my new method of personality typing: hot dogs.

First a disclaimer: Freud lived in Vienna, Austria. Hot dogs are often called wieners. Wiener in German means someone from Vienna. This relationship is purely coincidental. I can find no evidence that Freud ever ate a wiener. Freud did comment at length others who ate wieners but this too was coincidental I believe. I feel this disclaimer is necessary because I don't want any of you who choose to *peer-review* my scientific observations to suggest that I freeloaded from Freud and am, therefore, a fraud.

Some background: on a recent weekend my adult leadership volunteered me to cook hot dogs at the Oxford Community Center, Fine Arts Fair in our home town of Oxford, Maryland. My adult leadership was the cashier so there was no mooching: I ate 4 hot dogs in 2 days and paid for every one…at the time of eating and later. I had plenty of time, while gently rotating the tubular-comestibles on the Weber, to consider those purchasing the delicacies. Some might argue that my sample was skewed (I've never really understood skewing but I think it's something statisticians say to make their colleagues look bad) and that my population was of inadequate diversity to properly arrive at an analysis. I don't know what that means either but that's the way they talk in graduate school. My own observation is that a lot of different folks came to look at the art. People arrived on bicycles and a few arrived in exotic automobiles; most seemed to be ordinary folks, some were obviously uppity.

My job, in addition to whirling wieners on the Weber, was to sell the things. Now, as you might have noticed, the *I* in *INTJ* (see above) means introvert. I actually am. I have learned to survive in an extrovert world but I am an introvert. We won't delve too deeply into that: you'll just have to take my word for it. What I'm getting at though is that I can't sell squat. Introverts don't, as a rule, sell things. But I have adapted and pretend to be an extrovert sometimes. This is how I wound up selling hot dogs. Now an extrovert would just sell hot dogs and revel in the association with strange people coming by and kibitzing: I, however, analyzed.

Hot dogs really have a bad reputation. If you do a little research you discover that even in their earliest days folks were suspicious of the contents. Today we know that hot dogs are made of chicken-lips and pig posteriors. Way back, there was a suspicion that missing canines might have been included: ergo, hot dog. There are those who think hot dogs are entirely too pedestrian for their lofty status. Others say ingredients be damned and dive in…or on…to their enbunned beauties. As you can see, right there we have diversity.

Since this is a scientific paper, I think I need to tell you that I really like hot dogs. I have no qualms whatsoever regarding mystery ingredients. I like hot dogs made from fowl; I like them made with beef, I like them made with pork. I like hot dogs. My favorite meal when I'm on the road is a 7-11, quarter-pound *Big Bite* slathered in mustard and relish. Formerly, I put mayonnaise on my hot dogs but after 2 or 3 friends spontaneously threw up when they observed me do that, I stopped to protect my shoes. Now I only put mayonnaise on my hot dog when I'm alone or wearing rubber boots. Once I invited my adult leadership to a luncheon at the 7-11: she was less than impressed. So now, in my introverted fashion, I dine alone on my Big Bite and colossal-gulp, diet cola. So people like me got a higher approval rating in my analysis of people who eat hot dogs.

The baseline personality in my study was, indeed, me. There were many like me. They would approach the grill flashing a big grin and ask for 2 hot dogs, juicy. These people I will call *real people*. Real people received their dogs, promptly turned to the condiment table, slathered all types of embellishments on their buns and turned rapturous. To a person they looked heavenward, small trickles of hot dog juice running from the corners of their mouths, bits of relish adhering to their lips, mustard stains dotting their shirts. Vicariously I savored each bite with them. Real people wore old boat shoes, faded shorts, pull-over knit shirts and often had kids with them who ate hot dogs with the same delight.

At the other end of the continuum were uppity ladies (ULs) in matching designer shirts and slacks, with more gold on their hands than was mined in California during the entire Rush...diamonds big as horse apples. When offered a hot dog, their respective lips curled like window shades. A few said *no thanks* but most glared with a look that said, *You obviously don't appreciate who I am.* They were right.

A few I typed to be ULs had this peculiar look when I suggested a hot dog. Recognizing that look early on as one which said *I love hot dogs but I have ascended to uppityness and can eat nothing but caviar,* I said, paraphrasing the Las Vegas advertisement, *What you eat here, stays here.* Amazing responses: casting their culinary cautiousness to the winds, every one of this ilk asked for well-done hot dogs revealing a hidden taste probably not even known to their closest associations. They ate their dogs with their backs turned to the crowd but with the same gusto as the real people. I believe I saw a few, as they exited the food tent, look over their shoulders with a look of sincere appreciation. For a moment in time they were rescued from the world of uppityness and returned to the comfort of real people. *Go in peace.*

Well, there were a dozen or so other types that I will address when I present my paper to the National Association of Personality Typers in the fall. I expect to receive the Noble. What I can share, in summary, is that hot dogs, despite some awful publicity, remain the true American culinary delight. Displaced in society by the mere hamburger, a product, I believe, of pernicious advertising, the hot dog will soldier on. Those of us who love hot dogs, having been led to believe our enjoyment is akin to serial homicide, often eat alone, maybe in the cabs of our trucks, maybe in Lexuses parked in a dark cul-de-sac, but always savoring, enjoying, reveling. Turn back to your roots those of you who have gone uppity: there's a 7-11 nearby.

Of Nags and Scolds: *I wish some folks would just hush*

It seems every time I pick up the paper these days some scold is chastising somebody about something. I guess it's the times: presidential politics, a war, the economy, healthcare. It never seems to be a suggestion for something new; it always seems to be an attack on somebody for what they tried to do. These attacks are bad. Perhaps, in these days, the only thing that is bipartisan is the scolding…the attacks. Then there are the nags: they won't give up. They keep hammering away on some mundane issue about which nobody cares…just to keep the cameras on themselves.

I'm not a big *letter to the editor* kind of person. The old sci-fi writer Robert Heinlein said, *Never try to teach a pig to sing; it wastes your time and it annoys the pig.* I really try to live by that philosophy. A few months ago I succumbed to the urge to give porcine music lessons and wrote a letter to the editor. It was regarding an issue I felt strongly about. I expected there would be letters from a few who disagreed with my position: there were. And every one of those was scolding. Not a single one debated my position: every one attacked me. It seems that that is where we are in discourse today.

So that got me interested on the history of scolds: ever heard of the *ducking stool*? This was an early form of the contemporary torture method, the water board. Unfortunately, the ducking stool was a sexist device. It was used, primarily, for women. And primarily for women who were nags or scolds. I'm not going to get into early attitudes here but the device as a form of punishment for nags and scolds intrigues me. The male counterpart to the ducking stool was pillories and stocks. I can't find much evidence of men being punished for being nags and scolds but I'm sure there were plenty men who engaged in these obnoxious practices...they just got away with it. I did find one reference to a man being punished by ducking...he was a wife beater. The same reference said brewers of bad beer and bakers of bad bread were sufficiently unethical for punishment in the ducking stool.

Pillories are those things you see in the replica colonial villages and museums into the bottom half of which you put your arms and neck which are then confined by the lowering of the upper half. This would then be locked by the bailiff for the period of the prescribed punishment. Stocks were similar except they were locked around the ankles. Persons enduring this punishment then became the target for produce whose time in the garden had been excessive.

The purpose of the ducking stool and pillories and stocks was humiliation. Somewhere along the way, humiliation was determined to be inhumane…dehumanizing. Parenthetically, I don't see how this is any more dehumanizing than being locked up in a cell with a 250 pound bodybuilder who looks at you and says, *Hi, Honey*. Anyway, I'm proposing we bring back the ducking stool. And maybe pillories and stocks too. But, here's the kicker, we only use them for politicians.

Just think of the possibilities. We could build a ducking stool right down there on the Mall, alongside the reflecting pool. The Park Police could man it. Maybe the stocks and pillories could be in the same place. That way we wouldn't need so many Park Police…judging from crime against tourists in Washington, they're pretty shorthanded already. If a politician got locked in the pillories or the stocks, a vendor could sell rotten produce to interested citizens who would then have to pay a quarter for each toss. Shoot, we could repair the entire failing infrastructure in the country and fund a few pork-barrel projects too on the revenue from this enterprise. I mean look at the approval rating of Congress right now: I think people would line up in formidable queues to express their appreciation for the job their elected officials are doing.

Now, let's see: the ducking stool would be for politicians who stand up in one of the chambers and berate others. This is scolding and, if they don't knock it off and get to work, glug-glug. You know who I'm talking about. They never have any good ideas, all they can do is criticize the ideas of others. I'm being bipartisan here…they all do it. Time to make'm stop. And if they don't come up with a good idea every once in a while, that should get them a bath in the old rocking chair as well. They've got *sergeants-at-arms* in both the House and Senate, let them enforce this rule. *You haven't had a good idea in 6 months buddy, get your swimsuit.* The reason I think the *no-idea* rule should apply here is because when they don't have ideas all they do is scold others.

I'll bet you thought I'd forgotten the old mahogany manacles didn't you? Nope, those are for the nags. The nags are the politicians who just won't leave an issue that's been resolved alone. They keep having hearings and investigations and more hearings. You know the types. If you ask the same question enough, somebody is going to say something that will get them a perjury charge and the nags will then gloat. Gloating nags should spend twice as much time in the target zone. Once again, not a partisan issue: both sides of the aisle do it. There are a couple of politicians that come to my mind: I'd love to invest several roles of quarters to lob a few pommes d'amour in their direction.

Perhaps I'm being too narrow. Maybe we should expand this concept to other branches of government as well. People working for the executive branch who leak classified information which endangers the lives of our military might spend a week in the stocks eating nothing but tomato sandwiches and vegetable juice. Might be room there for some judges who have forgotten the law too.

Well, I'm not naïve: it ain't gonna happen. But you have to admit, if we had some way of telling those folks who actually took an oath to look out for our interests that they aren't …between elections…it would probably be pretty popular and might get a few of them motivated. Excepting their sexism, those old colonials seem to have had some pretty good ideas. I know, I'm just trying to make Miss Piggy sing arias.

Blowboaters' Revenge: *I have fun and everybody else gets mad*

I have it on good authority that the high cost of gasoline is not caused by excessive demand in China or India or the crisis in the Middle East: it is a contrived crisis generated by sailboaters, the blowboater crowd. The fuel shortage is the result of a conspiracy by the blowboaters to once and for all ensure go-fast boats never leave the pier. It's true: would I lie to you?

This all began with a failure. The *Mufflers and Manners* subcommittee of the highly secretive *Blowboaters' Revenge* committee reported that their mission was not accomplished. The subcommittee had but one challenge: to convince operators of go-fast boats that Sunday morning should be respected by stilling their eight-million cubic inches and creating no wakes. To their credit, the Mufflers and Manners group did their best, dressing in muscle shirts and carrying cans of Bud Light to establish their bona fides and hanging around outside Tiki Bars. Their task was too great, however. I think it was the clear nail polish that revealed to their quarry that they were blowboaters. Not a single go-fast operator took the bait. As punishment for not achieving his goal, the head of M and M, as it's called by the cognoscenti, has been sentenced to work for a season as a busboy at the Crab Claw restaurant in St. Michaels, Maryland where his duties will involve handling lines for arriving go-fast boats…those few still running.

Having failed to achieve the simple goal of quieting Sundays, the blowboaters were forced to go high tech. When not getting manicures, many of the blowboaters work at an agency on southwest corner of Fort George C. Meade, Maryland, that is, ostensibly, a wholly owned subsidiary of the *New York Times* but is still secret to the rest of us. Some elements of this agency have been involved in a surreptitious project, actually an ill-kept secret, which involves tapping the electronic ignitions of go-fast boats plying the placid waters of the Chesapeake, tapped without permission of the respective owners. To date, the data elements are limited. The only recognizable datum is a frequent rhythmic rocking of very short duration, a phenomenon that remains a mystery to the blowboaters. Some alarming moans and screams have also been detected but these are believed to be associated with the cost of fuel.

Having failed at infiltration and electronic observation, the blowboaters were forced to go international. Using their connections with the *New York Times…All the news that fits, they print….*the blowboaters released some totally fabricated information that they assured the *NYT* was sensitive and compartmented, the release of which might endanger the lives of Americans and, therefore, should never be published …automatically ensuring front-page above the fold. It had to do with a minor gas shortage.

Well, as we know, this one got out of hand. Prices of gas shot through the roof. The cost of fuel for a single mega-cube, go-fast trip from Baltimore to Annapolis and back approached a grand. The thunderous roar and tsunami sized wakes were reduced to whimpers and ripples. Dock bars everywhere were threatened by fire marshals as their seating capacity was greatly exceeded by marooned, go-fast operators, forced to forego their rolled and pleated, white vinyl captains' seats for the chipped and splintered, wooden captains' chairs of the bar: ignominy my friends, ignominy.

Well, to say this backfired is an understatement. Speculators got involved and the costs of a barrel of crude went through the roof. This was a totally unexpected consequence of a simple plan to beach the go-fast crowd on Sunday mornings. And what's worse, blowboaters had to pay more to keep their iron-jibs, the little putt-putt Japanese diesels that they surreptitiously rely on for their primary locomotion, running. A gallon of diesel suddenly cost more than a box of white wine.

Not being the type to miss an opportunity, blowboaters are moving rapidly to profit from the crisis. Several companies have been established to oversee mothballed fleets of go-fast boats. Reminiscent of the rivers full of old ships of yesterday, hundreds of silenced go-fast boats will be rafted up awaiting the day the alchemists turn water into fuel and they can again roar up and down the Bay, their wakes flipping small boats and eroding the shores. Vast rafts of marooned Scarabs and Donzis and Cigarettes will bob in the gentle wakes of blowboaters as they tack and jibe around the fleets. The voices of small children will be heard, actually heard, asking their coiffed and manicured sailor parents, *What are those boats over there where all those seagulls are roosting? Those, dear child, are the vestiges of a bygone era when a gallon of gas cost less than a glass of Pouilly Fuisse and the roar of massive engines could be heard from miles and miles away.*

Enterprising marina owners will buy up the go-fasts and beach them on cinderblocks, turning them into kitschy motels for blowboaters whose own craft lack adequate air conditioning. In the cool evenings they'll sit in cockpits of their sleek and silenced accommodations, sipping their wine and reminiscing about being nearly swamped by a boat such as the one on which they sit.

The semi-hippy, watercolor painters, in their white socks and rubber clogs, will park their SUVs near marinas to capture on canvas the almost-sunk, go-fast boats, long forgotten by their owners, most of whom have turned to NASCAR. Much like the old abandoned oyster buy-boats and skipjacks featured on so many easels, half-sunk go-fast boats will appear in art shows all along the Bay, their tattered cockpit covers hanging listlessly, their big engines rusting in the mud.

It is a sad thing this: so many dreams, so many dock lines. All because of a quest for a quiet Sunday morning. So many boats marooned...with cobwebs collecting in their gas tank vents. So many stories about the days when thunder on the Bay frightened small children and old folks and dozens boats raced in *poker runs* for the illusive Ace of Spades. Perhaps we will again see the gleaming white rockets, their bows lifting high as they spring from swell to swell. Perhaps the costs of fuel will again be within reach of the common person. Perhaps pigs will fly.

Fiber Fraud: *I tell why I am a regular guy*

Are you as confused as I am about fiber? Is it or isn't it good for you? First the heart people say if you don't eat fiber you might as well hang it up. Then they say they got it wrong, fiber's not that great after all. This is after I've consumed enough hay to keep a passel of cows smiling. Then they say you should only eat whole grains because they have fiber and fiber's good for you. And that's after they said fiber wasn't that good for you after all. See what I mean?

My adult leadership never heard the part about how fiber might not be that good for you after all. Everything we eat in our house has fiber in it. Even the ice cream is whole grain. My orange juice has so much pulp in you can eat it with a spoon. I have to spend fifteen minutes in the grocery store reading the label on the blinking bread package to make sure I've got the whole grain kind. You find that information on the little postage stamp sized label that lists the ingredients, the one that resembles the inventory of a chemistry lab. It's so small I have trouble reading it even with my cheaters on. And it can't just be *whole wheat*: it has to be *whole grain.* And when I get it home, it gets checked.

The bakeries are on to something here. Through advertising, they've got the entire country worried about irregularity. We are bombarded with advertisements about this indelicate subject. And now we've been convinced that bread with whole grain in it is good for us. Don't you see what's happening? The bakeries just take the grain right out of field, slap some binder on it and bread happens. They don't have to mill the stuff. Think of the money they save. All they had to do was tell us it's good for us and we fall right into place.

I don't believe in conspiracies because I don't think humans can keep secrets. All you have to do is read the papers lately and you see that in spades. This notwithstanding, I'm a little worried that there may, in fact, be a little collusion among the fiber folks. Those articles telling us about how if we didn't eat more fiber we'd wind up so bound up that our heart would quit were splashed right across the front page, above the fold. Where was the article about how fiber might not be so great? In the lifestyle section…and nobody reads that. Doesn't that make you wonder?

I don't want you to spend a lot of time sitting there thinking about constipation. It happens. That has to be the reason every night we're told dozens of times…fiber, fiber, fiber. They bombed on the fiber-heart connection so they've moved south. These marketing people are not dumb; their data has to be backed up. But regular folks have been led to believe that this is something that's inevitable: you will get constipated. Have you seen that ad featuring poor old Raymond? He's in the checkout line and his wife is ragging him about his *problem*. Talk about embarrassing. And then there are all those fiber pill adverts. Swallow one of those suckers and it inflates to a bale of hay inside your gut. That'll work things out for sure.

Cows eat a lot of fiber. If you've ever been around a bunch of cows, you know what fiber does to them. Fiber does the same thing to you. Oh yeah, it does. That's the dirty little secret the fiber folks don't tell you. They push their product touting all those benefits…and they don't tell you about greenhouse gasses. It may be that all this fiber we've been eating is the real reason the glaciers are melting. Think about it.

My wife likes to start my day with a big bowl of fiber. She creatively disguises it with strawberries and blueberries but it's still cow food. The manufacturers cleverly mold it into little shapes but I'm not fooled. That stuff is only a baby step from the threshing machine. It tastes like cardboard and has the texture of a cedar shingle. You can soak that stuff in milk for an hour and it's still rigid…not crunchy, rigid. But I'm told it's good for me and I know her heart's in the right place. And I am a regular guy; regular.

I was watching the Discovery Channel the other day: they had a program on the history of cereal. I had been thinking about this column so I thought the program might give me a little insight. Do you know who Kellogg was? He ran a spa up there in Michigan, the mission of which was to clean out his clientele. Seems he had a theory that bowel health led to health in other areas as well. He experimented with different compounds to feed his patients and, voila, breakfast cereal was invented. Dr. Kellogg became a very rich man and nobody ever said he was full of it.

Maybe Dr. Kellogg and some of those purveyors of fiber are right. Maybe the whole world is bound up. Might explain a lot about all the conflict we have. Perhaps a high fiber diet would solve a lot of international problems. The United States is the largest producer of cereal grains in the world. Think about it: if we could promote regularity through fiber as part of international diplomacy who knows what the outcome could be. Certainly our farmers would be happy. I can see diplomats sitting around discussing the future of the world, sipping on Metamucil, whole grain muffins in little baskets positioned around the table. Heck, we're halfway there: we had a Secretary of State named Rice.

The old folks used to believe in the *high colonic*. I don't know for sure how that's done but I think it involves a fire hose and some sort of chemical-based fluids. It was supposed to rid the body of toxins by hosing out the bowel. My mother, an otherwise well-educated woman, used to attribute all sorts of maladies to bowel toxins. And you know what that meant. We got a dose of some foul tasting stuff and had to stay home for the day. So I guess people have been attributing problems in the gut to problems elsewhere for a long time. Old Dr. Kellogg was searching for the truth when he invented corn flakes. Scientists still ponder the value of edible hay; they just haven't determined exactly what it is that edible hay is supposed to cure… and, in the meantime, convince you that you can't live without fiber. I'm going to continue to follow my adult leadership's advice and eat as much fiber as I can. I don't think it can hurt and the unfortunate side is a passing problem. Someday the scientists may discover that the world's diplomatic issues could be solved with a high fiber diet. That's great but it doesn't solve the problem of the glaciers.

The Tree Rat Wars: *Arboreal rodents are driving me nuts*

Indulge me for a moment. I need to say this: the blinking tree rats are driving me nuts. *What has this to do with life on Chesapeake Bay?* you might inquire. Well, I've done a survey. Nine out of ten people on our bay are sick of squirrels too. I limited my research to the street on which I live and, to be certain, the sample group was a bit sloshed at the time of inquiry: this notwithstanding, I believe my group voted honestly. They hate the little varmints. To a person they agree that the squirrel population is out of hand—except maybe for the little old lady who thinks they're cute and feeds them peanuts but she had passed out and didn't vote anyway.

When I was a kid, every squirrel in the woods knew my trusty four-ten shotgun and me. They had a little code where they banged hickory nuts and acorns together when we entered their habitat: at least I think that's why I seldom found any. The ones I did find wound up on the breakfast table, smothered in gravy and served over grits. (No, I will not tell you what a *grit* is. If you don't know, just wallow in your ignorance.)

Well, I grew up and the old four-ten got stuck in the back of the closet where it still resides.

I agreed to let the squirrels and other creatures of similar ilk do their thing and I would do mine. But now they have crossed the line. The little monsters have gone after my peaches.

Lately I have accepted the fact that some folks think I'm heartless. My position on the invasive mute swans has caused me to receive a little grief. That's okay: I think I'm fairly secure in my opinion regarding those nasty creatures. I've ignored the threatening phone calls. I don't believe the rumors that a gang of swans is waiting for me out on the Tred Avon River near my home, planning to sink my boat and flog me into turtle food. But I think my position on squirrels will resonate. Even the benighted swan fanciers, for the most part, will support my dislike for the beady-eyed little brush tails.

I have but one peach tree. I've been allowed to keep it in the garden even though it offends her horticultural majesty...it is inharmonious and occupies the moonbeam corner or some such fung shooie thing. I spray it and care for it. My friend Van who is an expert helps me keep it pruned. And it produces an abundance of peaches...that never grow to maturity. Why? You got it: the damned tree rats. They don't particularly like peaches as is evidenced by their habit of taking one bite of the immature fruit and then rejecting the remainder.

And they will do that until every last peach is gone from the tree.

I haven't always been so hard on the squirrels. For a while, I tolerated their fondness for my birdseed even though they chased away the cardinals I have been working hard to attract. When they got a little too greedy, I bought those feeders with the tricky little platforms that close when any weight larger than a cardinal presses on it. The feeders have made for some good, cheap entertainment as the bushy tails have tried to figure out how the beat the device. They haven't. But they don't give up easily. I have seen more than a few of them take a dive off the top of the feeder...and back they come. But when they go after my peaches, the entertainment stops.

So, what to do? I went to the Internet. You would not believe the web sites devoted to the problems of managing squirrels. I think there are more squirrel-war sites than there are sites for the war on terrorism. And an abundance of suggestions. One of my favorites is the tea made of cayenne pepper. Soak some of that flaky red pepper you sprinkle on your pizza and then spray the tea on your fruit. I tried red pepper on my birdseed before I got the tricky platform feeders: my squirrels are fond of red pepper. I think they were disappointed when I stopped seasoning the birdseed. So much for that idea. There were some others that I thought had merit.

My adult leadership and I were walking one day when we noticed a friend of ours ahead. He took a trap from the back of his car and headed over to a bulkhead on the side of the creek. I knew right away what he was doing and tried to divert my wife's attention. Look, I said, I think we are beginning to have an eclipse of the sun. Too late: she saw the squirrels. The creatures knew what was coming: they were headed for their last swim. I tried to persuade my wife that that end was better than frying on a power line, a customary local end for many, or being run over by a pickup. She still refuses to speak to that neighbor. I didn't tell her, but I thought he had a reasonable solution.

Cyanide was out. I couldn't shoot them, not in town. They prefer pepper. And they are really hard to herd so running them under the wheels of the garbage truck didn't seem to be a good solution either. My friend's trap: maybe I could trap them and dispose of them in a more humane way than seeing how long they could tread water. I bought a trap. Forty bucks for the trap and a dollar for three ears of dried field corn from my local purveyor of all things vegetal, Mr. Bill Eason, and I was ready. I felt like one of those khaki clad hunters in the old jungle movies. Couldn't find a pith helmet.

The humane trap is an interesting device. You put the bait, corn in this case, in the back of the trap. When the greedy little creature goes after the corn, it steps on a trigger and a spring-loaded door closes behind. I set up an observation post in my upstairs bedroom. Got my binoculars and a glass of iced tea and stood by. Didn't take long. There he was, sliding in under the hostas. He sniffed, dug a little at the back of the trap, rounded the front and went in. I had him. Jubilation!

Five bushy tails have been caught and transported. A friend of mine, who claims advanced knowledge of squirrels, says they have to be moved at least six and half miles or they'll return. Fine with me. I took them over near the town of Trappe...I enjoyed the irony. Wife suggested I daub their tails with a little orange paint, just in case they did return. I was afraid if I did that they might get lead poisoning or something and the phone calls would start again so I just fed them a little corn and transported them to a nice wood. Before releasing them though I looked them in the face. I said next time they better be wearing water wings.

Advice (Old vs New): *New boat or used*

There are few things as dear to those of us who love the water as breakfast. You know I'm right. Okay, maybe you're different. Maybe you prefer candlelight dinners or a *déjeuner* at some place that puts fancy gravy on everything. If you like that better than breakfast though you're probably one of those who judge a boat by how many people she'll sleep. For me breakfast ranks right up there with the feel of a good helm, the pull of a good fish, the smell of salt water and sunrises and sunsets on unbroken horizons.

I have a few special places where I like to eat my eggs, scrambled with cheese thank you, and drink my early morning coffee. One of those is in Deale, Maryland. You know the place. When I surveyed a boat down around Deale, I always allowed plenty of time for breakfast. It's nice being called *hon*, all the waitresses do that. Someday I'm going to devote an entire piece to that place, maybe a book. Gone now but my absolute favorite spot though was the Chatterbox Café, a few blocks from my house in Oxford, Maryland.

Every Saturday morning a bunch of us guys would meet at the Chatterbox for breakfast. The wives called our little klatch, *Scratch and Spit*. Hey, I heard that! We *were* politically correct and in touch with our... well, you know. We've often invited the ladies but, for some reason, they never seemed interested.

Scratch and Spit is a forum for really deep philosophical topics like the perennial question, *Should ketchup be allowed on scrapple when dining in polite company?* It was lost on my fellow philosophers that the question was moot, *nobody* eats scrapple in polite company. Scrapple is a greasy sausage thing made from chicken lips and pigs' tails. The Scratch and Spit bunch were not exposed to much polite company anyway. Politics and religion were fair game. That other subject came up to but most of us were too old to worry much about it.

The question one Saturday was whether to buy a new or used boat. This is a powerful topic this time of the year. The election is over. Scandals in Washington remain perpetual. Spring is in the offing. Boat shows are happening. People are thinking of buying boats. The topic of new or used always comes up. My breakfast buddies had strong arguments favoring both sides.

It seems the new-boat crowd likes the concept of breaking in the boat themselves. That way they have a clear history of how the vessel has been treated. There is a lot to be said for that. If you manage the break-in period properly and keep your engines serviced you can expect years of good performance. However, boat builders do have bad days: lemons happen.

The used boat cohort argues that a boat that's had a prior owner has all the bugs worked out of it. Well, that can be true. But there are those boat owners that didn't manage the break-in period properly.

I tried my best to stay out of this discussion but I was getting a headache trying to contain my tupence worth. When finally asked for my opinion, I pounced.

Boats are complex period. And volumes have been written about how to buy a boat. But there are a few basic principles that apply to the art and science of boat buying.

If you are shopping for a new boat, let's just use that term for both brand-new and *previously-enjoyed* for the moment; you've got to figure out what is the *right* boat for you. I know a lot of boat-savvy people on the Chesapeake Bay. They know boats and boating and suggesting that they don't know what boat suits them would get at least a nasty look. But maybe you're not as comfortable as these folks. Maybe you've been messing about in a little sloop or exploring the creeks in a skiff powered by a little putt-putt. Maybe you want something different. Maybe you're between boats. You have a right to ask that question.

What is the right boat for you? The answer is amazingly simple, at least in my humble opinion: the largest boat you can afford and are competent to operate, or, are willing to learn to operate safely. Why the biggest? In today's water world, safety is something we have to think a lot about more than we used to. There are too many people that ought to be watching from the pier out there operating boats. Bigger, assuming it is maintained and operated properly is safer. And make sure it has amenities that will please most everyone with whom you will go boating. Yes, you do have to consider where you're going to keep it: that comes under the *afford* category.

Now that we've decided you need a bigger boat, let's see if it should be new or well broken-in. I like new boats. They have a nice smell like a new car: none of that old mildew or holding tank odor. No old fuel fumes in the engine space. You can almost smell the shine. What could possibly be wrong with a new boat? Not much actually. I do, from time to time, see boats that are poorly assembled. In the old days, it was not uncommon to see a deck peeled away from a hull because of a poor hull-to-deck joining. Companies whose names you probably would recognize have gone bankrupt paying for repairs to boats poorly designed or badly built. Today, most manufacturers are adhering to nationally recognized, recommended boat-building standards and things are better. But you still need to be aware. Do your homework. Ask around. Don't buy a boat from the Zippy Boat and Awning Repair Company that may knock off a hundred or so boats and then disappear. Buy a boat built by a company with a good reputation, which adheres to recommended boat building standards. You know who they are. If you don't, your friends do. Use the Internet. Do extensive research.

The two most important points to consider when buying a new boat are warranty and depreciation. If you choose to buy new, check on the company that is selling the boat. Find out the experiences others have had. If they don't take care of their customers, don't honor their warranties, go to the folks that do. Your lawyer and your boat dealer do not need to know each other. Depreciation is the cost of the shine on all that new stuff. It is the premium you pay for new and you pay it almost as soon as you sign the check. Some folks think that near-instant loss in value is worth it. You decide.

If you choose to buy a used boat, apply the same considerations you would if buying a brand-new one: find a boat whose name you know, whose reputation is good, and one for which you don't have to hire a private detective to find a dealer. I know there are some new boat builders out there that seem to be turning out a good product. You have to decide if you want to be part of the *new-product test group*. Again, do your research.

I think here is where I have to put in a plug for surveyors. Even if you know everything there is to know about boats, it helps to have a disinterested opinion. Replacing the transom or engine bed because the encapsulated wood is rotted can cost a lot more than a survey. The *little* electrical job done by the boat's previous owner can become a *big* problem for you. Rigging does fail on sailboats. I have seen repairs poorly done but very well camouflaged. I have amazed more than one *expert* who didn't catch something that showed up when we surveyed the boat. Choose a surveyor who is known to you or your friends or who is certified by the National Association of Marine Surveyors (NAMS) or accredited by the Society of Accredited Marine Surveyors (SAMS). That will go the furthest in assuring you get a competent surveyor.

The *rule of thumb* for such things says the vessel's propulsion system is forty-percent of the boat's value. I agree with that: it might even be conservative considering the value of today's outboards and engines. The *eyeball test* will tell you a lot. Is the engine, lower unit, or outdrive dirty, rusty, or corroded? Be suspicious of new paint on engines and outboards: look for paint overspray on the hoses. What do the hoses look like? What do the bellows look like? Is there black soot in the exhaust outlets or on the topsides or transom?

You should do a seatrial: the garden-hose run-up is never enough. Take the boat out and run the heck out of it. On planing hull boats, you should be able to achieve plane from a standing start with wide-open throttle in 4 to 5 seconds. Engines shouldn't bog down on hard turns. Can she back down? Are there clunks and clanks, backfiring and hesitation? What color is the exhaust smoke and how much is there? There are lots of ways a scoundrel can hide engine defects: temporarily. I think a few hours of a good mechanic's or engine surveyor's time could be one of your better investments. Have them along on the seatrial. May turn out that your propulsion system is pristine: may turn out that you have to spend several hundreds of dollars, or more, before you can enjoy your new boat the first time.

My Scratch and Spit buddies regretted that they ever asked me the question. My eggs were cold. And I needed more coffee. But these things are important to you and me. Go forth and get your new boat. And enjoy.

Arsters and Oistas: *I ignite a family feud*

It's those blasted bivalves. They get me in trouble every year. I try to stay neutral. I try to stay out of the fray. I endure. I behave. But I always get trapped. I've done the research; oysters in the Chesapeake Bay and oysters in Apalachicola Bay, Florida, are the same critters--*crassostrea virginica* if you insist. But every year, around Memorial Day, I suffer yet another humiliating attempt to convince me otherwise.

For those of you who are not that familiar with the geography of the South, Apalachicola Bay is a little indentation on the Gulf Coast of Northwest Florida. It happens to be about sixty miles or so from my family home in Tallahassee. I'm blessed with four brothers and a brother-in-law, who is more brother than in-law, who are convinced that Apalachicola Bay oysters are different than those we harvest on the beautiful Chesapeake; better they say and they will bet on it. And they are obsessed with convincing me of this proposition.

This all got started when I chose to drop my anchor in Maryland rather than return to Florida. My wife and I considered all the arguments and Maryland won. No regrets. But to that bunch down south, this was close to treason. And somehow, the poor oyster has become the symbol of my betrayal. Around Memorial Day those of us who can gather at my sister's in Tallahassee for a reunion. And another skirmish in the oyster war begins.

I love oysters: raw, stewed, roasted, anyway they can be made available. A little more than a block from my house, watermen unload their harvest: baskets of the beautiful bivalves, glistening and beckoning, *Take me home. Have your way with me!* I swear my truck pulls to that side as I pass. But I persevere. Usually. After all, I know what too many oysters will do to you. I'm already bald.

To hear that bunch down south though, Chesapeake Bay oysters are nothing more than a loogie on a half-shell. No self-respecting oyster, or *oista* in their parlance, would grow outside Apalachicola Bay they rant. No amount of persuasion can counter their efforts at dissuasion. I try though.

On our family beach trips when I was a kid, we would see the watermen in their skiffs, their hand-tongs wigwagging as they scratched the bottom, grubbing after the next clump just like you might see them here.

Even in the R-months in North Florida, it gets hot out on the water. I'm sure the struggle against the heat is only exceeded by the struggle to earn a living in a business that knows very little wealth. The distinctive skiff of Apalachicola Bay, with its upswept sheer, shares with its Chesapeake Bay counterpart a very small cabin, barely adequate for refuge when the squalls come thundering in off the Gulf. I'm partial to oysters taken from the waters off Eastpoint, not far from the village of Apalachicola. Off Eastpoint you see a small flotilla of skiffs bobbing in rhythm to the tonging of their waterman.

Part of our family beach trip ritual was oysters. My dad would buy a half-bushel in a croaker sack – a burlap bag to most of ya'll – and stow them in a cooler under ice. The anticipation of the treat was so great, my brothers and I would stop harassing each other for a while.

My mother could never tolerate raw oysters. Her description of a raw oyster was a biological reference that would pause the most dedicated oyster lover. She chose to make the stew. I think we had to put aside every third oyster we shucked for her. Sauté fresh oysters in butter, add cream, milk and seasoning: simple and simply delicious. In my house you would never see those fancy little round oyster crackers. No way. Saltines, the bread of life in the South, were the only cracker allowed.

When the family gathered for oysters, the process was always the same. Dump the oysters in a bushel basket and hose them off. Oyster knives, spikes, the ends of which my grandfather had flattened and ground, were passed around. A fire built in the old barbeque fashioned from a fifty-five gallon drum was allowed to burn down to a bed of glowing embers. My grandfather, father, uncle, brothers, and cousins, and myriad friends would stand around eating oysters raw or roasted over the coals, washing them down with hyper-sweetened iced tea - no beer in that old Baptist family.

I remember how happy I was when I learned how to shuck my own oysters so I didn't have to wait for some adult, who was usually busy satisfying his own interests, to open a few for me. I have a little scar below my thumb on my left hand that is my badge of honor – evidence of the slipped oyster knife. Only real oyster lovers have those.

When the mosquitoes got too thick or the stew was ready, whichever came first, the lot would retreat to the kitchen and victory mugs full of oyster stew. My grandmother's banana pudding would finish the feast.

You're beginning to see what I'm up against aren't you. That Tallahassee crowd grew up with oysters from Apalachicola Bay. Provincial though they are, you can sort of appreciate their position. After all, I went away. Far away. As far as they are concerned, anything north of Georgia might as well be in another country. No, they aren't dumb, just proud of what they've got. When I come back home and mention that I had an absolutely delectable plate of Chesapeake Bay *arsters* it rankles them some.

Now I don't mean to be provocative. When I describe the succulence, the tang, the fatness of the oysters of Chesapeake Bay, they just seem to get argumentative. I explain that I get them just down the street, right off the boat, barely minutes from the first bite of the waterman's tongs, so they have to be good. The Florida crowd has to go sixty miles to get them that fresh. I point out that the relative coolness of the Bay contributes to their superior flavor. Bay oysters don't have to endure the hot soup of the Apalachicola shallows on their way to the plate. My siblings start to act as though they've been soaking in something hot.

I'm really not intending to antagonize my brothers. I wouldn't do that. I mean, look, I've just got a special circumstance. I've had both the northern and southern varieties of whatever that Latin name was. How can their opinions be respected about the better oyster when all they have tasted is the southern example?

After I've played with 'em for a while, I let them off the hook. Okay, I say, I'll allow that the best oysters available in Tallahassee are from Apalachicola Bay. And when I'm home during the season, I enjoy every one of them I can get.

Oistas ain't *arsters*, never mind their Latin connection. I can get *arsters* most of the time in season and I gotta tell you, you can't beat'em. When I'm back home with my family and the iced tea pitcher has streams of sweat running down its sides, and you can smell the stew in the making, *oistas* aren't bad at all.

Note: It was my habit when writing my columns to send manuscript copies to family and special friends. They were good at spotting typos or instances where I just goofed. When this copy was dispatched to the special group, brother Alan wrote a rebuttal and sent it to the editor…who did not tell me until my article and the rebuttal were published. Sheesh!

Wino Demographics: *For those with thirst for information*

I have a bunch of friends for whom wine has become a problem. No, I don't mean they're hanging out by the soup kitchen with a half-consumed bottle of Ripple, its threaded neck peeking out from a khaki sack. I'm concerned that they might start spending too much time analyzing wine and not enough time quaffing. Me, I'm a quaffer: ain't got time to analyze.

I live in a town where wine consumption is ten times the national average. We have tank trucks that come in and offload the stuff into ceramic vessels of about 500 gallons capacity, kept at perfect temperatures: whites at 50, reds at 65. Vacuum pumps suck out the harmful oxygen and nitrogen is pumped in to keep the wines from rusting…well, oxidizing anyway. The location of these tanks is kept secret and the trucks delivering the juice are marked heating oil.

Actually, that's just a fantasy I had after consuming too much Italian wine with a name that resembles that of a cookie. Really though, this crowd in my town does drink a lot of wine. Normal menu planners say one bottle per couple for a dinner party: that'd make you a laughing stock around here. The garbage truck had to put on a set of those extra wheels you see on dump trucks to take the weight from all the bottles on a typical weekend.

My study of local wine consumption has revealed some interesting demographics. There are those who like to fondle wine but seldom drink it; those that drink a lot of wine and fondle it; and those that don't give a rat's patootie about the origin of the liquid as long as it has some relation to berries and has alcohol. I'm a wino somewhere between the second and third tier, depending on how late it is in the evening.

My friends are not fondlers: analyzers not fondlers…at least not yet: fondlers are also called wine snobs. They buy wines and store them in stone caves, air conditioned by exotic equipment, the cost of which could support a comfortable retirement. They have dusty old bottles that are biblical in origin. Fondlers know the pedigree of each bottle. They are likely to tell you the age of the vine from whence came the grape, the composition of the soil in which it was grown and the weather report for the entire twelve-months before the grape was harvested. And they are likely to tell you. And tell you. And tell you. Fortunately, I don't know any winos of the snobby ilk.

I used to know a wine snob: fact is, he was my former father-in-law. Prior to meeting him I was perfectly happy with a jug of Gallo. There's irony in that. Probably would never have proposed marriage to his *perfect* daughter had I not been under the influence of some *Hearty Burgundy*. The Bible's right, that stuff can ruin your day. See, it was a little motel down in Virginia Beach and the evening was nice and the wine wasn't bad and…well, sierra happens. Former father-in-law never quite liked me and I attribute that to my plebian tastes in wine. But he did endeavor to educate me on matters enological and for that I'm grateful. He'd buy some good stuff and I didn't mind the learning experience at all.

One of my more pleasant wine drinking experiences was when I was living in Germany courtesy of your hard earned tax dollars. If I haven't before, I thank you for that. Did a lot of skiing and drank some good wine. I lived not far from the French military PX. For the incognoscenti, a PX is like the company store. I was always told the French didn't give a hoot for the military side of NATO but their presence in Germany said something a bit different. Anyway, the French were there in considerable numbers. And they had a PX that had barrels of wine, literally. You held your jug under the spigot and filled her up: white or red…actually, a couple of varieties of each. Not being a frogophone, I was dependent on the daughter of the aforementioned wine snob to translate...she did good. Those were some excellent wines for fifty-cents a gallon. The French clerk did sniff a bit when we checked out but I think she had a cold.

Which brings me back to my demographic analysis. With very little effort, you can get some good wines on the cheap. That's what my buddies are up to. Which is not to say they haven't invested in some expensive vino too...have to keep reminding them to keep their feet firmly planted. But the real fun is to find good wines for which you don't have to get a second mortgage. And they're out there.

We've discovered what was discovered on the Left Coast a long time ago: Trader Joe's. Maryland's screwy alcoholic beverage laws seem to have prevented Trader Joes's from selling wines in Maryland so you have to go to another state if you want to score some good stuff...wine that is. Everybody seems to have heard of *Two-Buck Chuck*. Well, that's TJ's *Charles Shaw* label. It's good and it's cheap. I've never seen it for two-bucks but it doesn't cost much more than that. They've got some other brands too that we buy for our wine rack. Their *Purple Moon* label offers several different varieties. I've been assured that the *Purple Moon* has nothing to do with the way they crush the grapes.

A lot of gourmet magazines and wine aficionado publications have recommendations for good, bargain-priced wines. It's fun to find those and try them. It's amazing where they'll turn up. Occasionally, you find some in the good old grocery store. What's really remarkable is when you read about some good, inexpensive wine available for five or six dollars a bottle and it shows up for ten-bucks a glass in the local *Bistro Effete*.

My friends who are analyzing are experimenting with cellaring wines too. I'm going to keep an eye on them. If they begin to look like fondlers, we may have to have a *Two-Buck Chuck* intervention. I'm not terribly worried though: they have the right demographics.

When you hear the term *wine tasting* you usually picture some dude with a mauve, paisley ascot, pinky extended, talking about an impudent little wine with aromas of frangipani and old oak or something like that. But you don't have to go to those shows for a fun wine tasting. If your wine demographics are right, you can have a bunch of fellow winos over for a good stew and just savor the varieties: no ostentation, no fondling, no pointing pinkies allowed. No searching for abstruse adjectives: just a lot of fun.

Dog Breath and Other Delights: *Or why I love my dogs*

Gary Larsen's last *Far Side* cartoon was printed in 1995. I loved the *Far Side* cartoons. In actual fact, they're still available in books but that's not the same as a fresh cartoon daily. One of the frequent subjects at which Larsen chose to poke fun was dog breath. Perhaps there are among you a few who have never enjoyed a Larsen cartoon. Go to the library. He's a hoot. And he made dog breath funny.

Those of you who read these words with some regularity might recall that our house belongs to two yellow labs: Sean and Paddy. Paddy owns the downstairs. His hips are bad and the stairs aren't worth it. He sleeps on the couch in the family room, thank-you very much. Sean, however, ascends the stairs with gazelle-like alacrity. His bed is the best L.L. Bean has to offer courtesy of his mother, my adult leadership. The bed is positioned on the floor at the foot of our bed. Sean snores.

Sean is a watch dog. No, he's not part of the security system: he's damn near afraid of everything. He's a watch dog because he keeps perfect time. Five o'clock in the morning is when his alarm, secreted somewhere in his golf-ball-sized brain, goes off. Mind you, most mornings at five o'clock I'm slumberating at near coma level. All of a sudden I start dreaming that I've been cast into the pit where the highway department throws the road-kill deer and it's mid August. Sometimes I dream that I've slipped and fallen into a fish house dumpster. Somewhere deep inside my comatose cephalous something is screaming *wakeup*. One eye pops open and all I see are lab teeth and pink tongue. All I smell is perfectly aged crab bait.

Brother Patrick, Paddy, has perfected this gambit as well. Being of the nap-requiring age, I'm inclined, on extremely rare occasions, to take a little refreshing siesta on Paddy's couch…the aforementioned family room dog bed. Paddy thinks I'm there to: 1) take over his bed; 2) get him a cookie; 3) go for a walk. He knows to wait until I start snoring, a sound I'm told resembles the compression brake on an eighteen-wheeler. Perhaps that should be 4) *that noise is hurting my sensitive dog ears.* Anyway, his breath is so powerful he doesn't have to get as close as his brother Sean: a couple of feet do the trick. When I was a young navy corpsman, I had the pleasure of sailing aboard troop transport ships with hundreds of marines. I don't want to get too specific; my adult leadership has run up the caution flag. So imagine a berthing compartment, where the marines sleep for you incognoscenti, with say a hundred, two hundred seasick marines. My job, among other things, was to keep them from getting dehydrated. Get the picture? That's what that Paddy-breath-in-the-face reminds me of. That's nostalgia I don't need. I'm immediately alert, give him back his bed, get him a cookie, take him for a walk, and stop snoring. He's happy. I go wash my face.

Do you know about *greenies*? These are green dog chews that are supposed to prevent bad dog breath...hound-a-tosis. Could you put out an oil well fire with a three-pound fire extinguisher? Slap a buzzard with a fly swatter? Put a saddle on a moose? We've gone through bags of those things...bupkis. Then the adult leadership reads that if they don't chew them properly, their little tummies can get upset. You know what's worse than dog breath? Soupy presents in the carpet in the morning, bad regardless of which end of the dog it came from; worsened by stepping in it on the way to the bathroom to rid yourself of that horrific pain in the lower abdomen. Do you know how badly your bladder can hurt when you're bouncing along on one foot because the other foot is encrusted with some evil substance best not called by its colloquial name in a family newspaper? I do. Greenies can do that. You have been warned.

Straying a bit from the breath subject, Sean is allergic. No, I didn't phrase that incorrectly. I didn't intend to say, *allergic to…* . He's allergic. The *to* part is darn near everything: trees, shrubs, grass, his momma's perfume, Heineken. I made up that last one but it wouldn't surprise me if I poured the boy a bottle, he'd break out in hives. So he's been prescribed *cyclosporine*. Sound familiar? If you've had a heart transplant it probably does. That's the medicine you get to keep you from rejecting your replacement ticker. And yes, it costs a bundle. And it causes the squirts. And no, he won't breathe in my face and say *Dad, I've got to go out.* No, he saves the breath thing for the morning. On these occasions when he has the tummy rumbles, he goes to the front bedroom, reads *Dog World* and leaves me a soupy present. To counter this, we go for a walk before turning in. He enjoys those walks…rain, sleet, snow, dust storm…we meander along, sniffing the respective *pee-mail* left by his friends. I keep saying, *Are we there yet?* He says he'll let me know.

Paddy loves his brother. Well, he's his adopted brother. He particularly loves his brother's poop. I know, about half of you just switched to the article on rockfish. But this is a treatise on dogs so you get the good dog/bad dog assortment. Labs are creatures of very bad habits. Poopy snacks are among the worst. It embarrasses Sean. He won't do that part of his business if his brother's around.

Sean goes outside to do his business and Paddy starts to drool. Paddy's fond of Canada goose droppings too. Do you think this habit might contribute to his breath problem? Goldfish as pets do have some redeeming qualities.

Sean went to see the doctor. Sean does that often…the allergies. An inspection of his choppers by the veterinarian elicited the observation that Sean had some gum problems. So Seancie got to have his teeth cleaned. The problems were minor but…Sean needs his teeth brushed regularly. And, of course, if Sean is getting attention, Paddy demands it too. I will not brush dog's teeth. Don't get you skivvies wedged, the adult leadership willingly took on the task. I get to clean up all the other stuff so I don't think this particular division of labor is inappropriate. Imagine for a moment: you hop out of bed, grab your toothbrush and squeeze out a nurdle…it is too a word…of good, old, chicken flavored toothpaste. How's that grab you? Me too. Thought of hurling. Dogs love it. Does nothing for the breath. The adult leadership has been assiduously brushing the fido-fangs and smearing on some kind of protective cream to boot. At least we might save some vet bills. Yuck! I'd rather step in something.

So Bunky, you ask why we keep the critters around. This morning, while drinking my coffee, sitting on the family room couch (see *dog bed* above), both dogs climbed up next to me and curled up, making sure at least some part of their anatomy was in contact with mine. Last night Sean, in our bedroom, slept most of the night with his head on my shoes. When I came downstairs this morning early, Sean tagging along behind, Paddy was waiting, tail going flat out. I got slurpy kisses and so did Sean. That's why. I don't care about the breath, the allergies, the bad habits, the vet bills, the millions of tons of blond lab, dog hair that I vacuum up six times a week. They make me exceedingly happy. They truly do love me and their human mother. You tell me where else you'll find that. I'm looking for a gas mask though.

Note: We lost Paddy in 2009. Sean's new brother Clancy, now 7, is a good dog too.

Ancestors: *I know who they are and I'm proud of them...mostly*

Has the genealogical bug bit you? Seems like most everyone I talk to is interested in knowing where they came from. Some have done some serious research; others, like me, have sponged off the work done by relatives. I'd always wondered if my daddy was telling the truth when he said most of our relatives were pimps and horse thieves. With a pedigree like that, I wasn't sure I deserved a place in polite society. So I bought some software, *Family Tree Maker* actually, and sallied forth. I didn't find any records of brothel managers or rustlers, but I sure did find some interesting characters.

Family legend had it that we were somehow related to Ireland. That's good: I like Ireland, particularly the stout libations emanating from the Emerald Isle. I knew about potato famines and Ellis Island and sort of figured somebody way back had stowed away and popped up in the big city saying here I am, America look out. I'd heard about Scots-Irish but really didn't know...or even care to know...much about them. Some family theorists had our name, Dial, as a variant of Doyle: suited me. My father had paid fifty bucks for a *coat-of-arms* many years ago that proclaimed that some ancient relative lived near a sun-dial; ergo, the name. The coat-of-arms was pretty extravagant as I recall, with plumbers' plungers errant with a sinister chicken and crossed dinner forks. At least that's what I remember it looked like. All those *sinister* and *errant* things are *coats-of-arms* talk. Well, my lucubration revealed that that was a heck of a long way from the truth and my pop was out a fifty.

Jim Webb, the former senator from Virginia, wrote an interesting book regarding the Scots-Irish, among whom he considers himself. Entitled *Born Fighting: How the Scots-Irish Shaped America* (highly recommended by the Bill Dial Book Club), Senator Webb explained why the Ulster Scots...the Scots Irish...grew tired of British persecution and came to America. Here they were exploited by the coastal aristocracy, many British, who gave them land on the frontier...nose to nose with the irate Indians who didn't have a whole lot of truck for the British either...and didn't know a Scotsman from a *Liverpudlian*.

Turns out my first ancestor in the colonies was Jeremiah Dalzell...pronounced *dee-el*. He was Presbyterian and a Scot...not Irish, not Scots-Irish...at least that's what I've read they considered themselves. He was born in Belfast but his family origins were in the lowlands of Scotland along the border with England. The Anglicans and the Catholics of dominant England had some difficulty with Presbyterianism and those they didn't kill were forcefully moved in massive numbers to Northern Ireland. Jim Webb says the hatred for the British by the Ulster Scots was profound. I believe this suited old Jerry Dalzell. He and his friends and family had been trying to make a go of it in Ireland with the flax and linen trade. The Brits, always willing to squeeze a little harder, began playing funny games with rents and taxes. This coupled with the way their families had been treated in Scotland, did not engender a lot of affection among the Ulster Scots for King and Crown. Jeremiah's preacher got a little put out with the British attitude and chartered five ships and moved his entire parish to South Carolina. Reverend William Martin must have been a heck of preacher to uproot an entire parish and transplant them across the Atlantic.

When Jerry and his fellow Presbyterians set up shop in South Carolina in 1772, things were getting a little funky in the colonies and the British were the cause of the smell. Up in Boston, men whose names are emblazoned on every important document we cherish were engaged in *committees of correspondence*. They were not writing love notes to the King. I doubt seriously that old Jeremiah Dalzell could read and write: that's something the preachers did. But I suspect he had a strong sense of politics. Jim Webb asserts that this is a characteristic of the Scots-Irish culture. I suspect Jerry and his fellow parishioners were pretty up-to-speed on the colonial happenings. I know that when the fighting finally broke out, Jerry and his boys took up arms…and I'll bet they didn't need a lot of persuading.

When I started my genealogical pursuits, I found that some family member a couple of generations back had designs on membership in the Daughters of the American Revolution. It was her interests that caused all the work to be done from which I profited. She got her membership. Pension records show that both Jeremiah and his son John were patriots. Jeremiah provided provisions, by this time he was a little old to do much trooping and shooting, and John was a sergeant in one of the outfits fighting with Francis Marion, the *Swamp Fox*. John was my grandfather, five grandfathers back. Francis Marion and his boys kicked some British backside.

The Mississippi Territory was opened for settlement in 1798. Lots of the Scots-Irish settlers on the East Coast looked west with interest in land touted as so rich anything would grow. The family Dial, the Dalzell moniker had become the victim of phonetics, loaded their wagons and set out. Jeremiah and John died before the family moved and are buried in South Carolina. The family settled in what is now western Alabama.

Somewhere along the way they all became Baptists…ostensibly because Baptist preachers were more abundant than Presbyterian.

I think it was after they arrived in Alabama that the pimps and horse thieves rumors got started. I don't have any records to support those activities but I do know there were some characters. One, whose wife had died, married a slave. I think they were happy because the relationship was productive. That relationship has been the subject of much speculation in the contemporary press so we won't go there. Another died after being kicked in the head by a mule. When the War Between the States (or *The War of Northern Aggression* as it's known where I come from) started, every ambulatory Dial of the appropriate age joined the Alabama forces. Jim Webb says that's what Scots-Irish do. They have a strong sense of loyalty…sometimes to their detriment. And they're willing to fight for causes they believe in.

I think, by identifying my roots, I feel better about myself. If I had discovered my first American ancestors arrived by steamer in New York harbor I would have been just as proud. It is kind of nice though to know that my old relatives believed so strongly in their causes that they would leave what they knew best and reestablish themselves across oceans of both water and culture. Jim Webb's book refined that even further. Us Ulster Scots are a tough and faithful bunch. When you look at my family, you can see that in spades. My four brothers and I are all retired military. And my sister, I sometimes think, is a sergeant major…but sweet.

Boatyards Goodbye: *It makes me a little sad*

I stopped by the Itty Bitty Boatyard of the Eastern Shore the other day to see my friend Hogan, the yard boss, and mooch some of his fresh coffee. Hogan keeps his Starbucks beans in a Maxwell House can so his friends won't think he's uppity. *Better enjoy that coffee while you can. Soon you won't get nothing but lemonade here,* he said with a sour expression on his leather face. I know better than to ignore Hogan when he leads with one of these comments…and I might want another cup of coffee. *And why's that?* said I.

Cause they're gonna turn the yard into one of those fancy marinas with the swimming pool and the tennis court and such. Everybody here's gonna have to leave. 'Cept for piddly little jobs, won't be any yard work done.

What'll they do with the regulars like Miss Violet and old George? Violet's a waitress down at the Snug Harbor, best place to get breakfast on the Eastern Shore. Lives in an old fiberglass houseboat that hasn't been away from the pier in fifteen years. Grows pretty red geraniums in old plastic buckets. George lives in a sagging old wooden motoryacht that he's been restoring for at least ten years. Does little jobs for Hogan. *They gotta be out*

of here by the end of next month, Hogan snarled.
We been trying to help 'em find someplace ...no
luck yet. We'll have to take a chainsaw to
George's boat.

Well, I haven't been this bummed out since
the hog ate the kittens. I've seen more good
boatyards turned into hoity-toity *yachtaramas* than
I care to think about. Old fashion boatyards, where
you can keep your boat in the water or out back
and not worry about what she looks like or how
long it takes to fix 'er up are anachronisms. Big
companies whose bosses probably get seasick near
a gravy boat are scooping 'em up and cleaning 'em
out. Most boatyards, naturally, are on the water.
The value of anything on the water seems to have
gone up faster than the space shuttle. Little
operations like the Itty Bitty can't fight off the
developers. And the costs of running boatyards
have soared just as high.

Wasn't that long ago, if you needed new
bottom paint on your old bateau, you just ground
off anything that didn't look good and rolled on
some fresh. Not anymore. Sanding dust is treated
like nerve gas or something. Folks in Washington
that don't know the difference between a barnacle
and belaying pin want you to crawl around on your
knees and collect little flakes of antifouling paint
with tweezers and deposit them in a special
receptacle. Old bottom paint has to be sealed in

lead lined containers and shipped with an armed escort to Yucca Mountain or someplace.

Volatile organic compounds, also known as *VOC*, are what most of us call fumes. Never been to a boatyard that wasn't fumy. But now we have to capture those fumes. I'm not talking about a yard hand with a pith helmet running around with a modified dustbuster here. The filtering systems required to capture VOC are big, expensive, and require skill to operate. The little boatyard can't begin to afford equipment like this. And what about the guy who's out back sheathing his boat with glass and resin to try and get a few more years out of her? He's going to be in real trouble if he runs afoul of the fumes police.

No one is more concerned about the environment than I am. And I believe those escaping VOC are probably doing damage to our atmosphere. It just makes me sad to see small boatyards go under because they can't afford to keep up with the requirements laid on them by people who've never set foot in a boatyard and probably look down their bureaucratic noses at those of us who do.

I've got a friend down in Florida who is worried about the one-ton manatee that lives most of the year off his pier. He's fairly certain the poop cops are going to descend on him and require a diaper for that sea cow. He has seen what the authorities have done to boats and surely that big critter produces more effluent than most of us. And he can't shoo the darned thing away either— protected.

Boatyards have to maintain expensive sewerage systems to deal with holding tanks on boats. And if they don't have the systems or can't afford them, somebody in a honey truck has to come by and suck up what they've collected and haul it off—for a fee. I agree we need to contain this stuff before every last oyster in the Chesapeake Bay dies of some horrific disease caught from what us humans got rid of. I'm just telling you, the boatyards are straining to keep up with all the requirements laid on them and feel, generally, that it is deserving of the same name as the substance in the holding tank.

I've listened to Hogan and his peers and they're getting killed. They can't afford all the technology that's required of them and they can't get the skilled help for a reasonable wage to operate it. And the developers are outside the gate salivating over the prospect of acquiring more waterfront.

If I owned a small boatyard and some slick dude in his BMW came by and offered me a couple of million for my four acre boatyard, I'd have to think long and hard. Sure, the folks that have kept their boats there for what seems like forever will be displaced. Sure all the slips will be emptied while the renovation takes place. And back there where George has his old Matthews, replanking her between paydays, they will want to dig the pool and put in the tennis court. I'd have to think about that. And that filter system the fume cops want installed back of the paint shed, I'd have to think about that too. And I'd probably walk away from my boatyard. And boatyard owners all over the place are taking hikes.

Makes me sad when I go to survey a boat in some place that used to be a neat little boatyard and now is all pastel and umbrellas. I miss the fumes and they sound of sanders and the smell of burnt coffee in the yard office. I miss old boatlifts with worn out tires and old motoryachts somewhere between derelict and a dream. There will never be a swimming pool in a marina that offers as much fun as diving off the end of a pier.

Catastrophe : *An evil creature moved in*

Has it ever occurred to you that there are some really negative words that begin with *cat*? For example, catastrophic, cataclysmic, catatonic...like that. I don't think that's coincidence. I think there's this subconscious thing about felines. Probably goes back to the saber tooth tiger days: fear of felines permanently imbedded in our cerebral circuits. I can understand why people might feel that way. I have a seven-pound, saber tooth that lives under my bed, beady eyes, fangs and all.

This all started when my adult leadership starting volunteering at the Humane Society Shelter. I knew the danger of this and expressed my concern that she might drag something home. I envisioned her showing up with some animal that was half dead, probably been hit by a semi and missing major portions of its anatomy...but still cute: she's like that she knows what a sucker I am for animals and, after a suitable protest, would welcome the poor critter. But she didn't do that. No. The thing she brought home is plenty healthy, claws, teeth and attitude in the top one-percent.

I've always been fond of cats. But I've always thought of them as heartbreakers. About the time you make friends with one, it'll scoot out the door and under the wheels of a dump truck and then you have to go out with a spatula and roll the thing up for suitable burial: breaks your heart. Actually, we had that happen once, sort of. Poor kitty got hit by a car and it died on our front walk. It was sort of mangled and I was impressed that it managed to get that far. I knew to whom it belonged and assumed he would want the remains for appropriate interment or whatever. I put it in a really nice Weejuns box and laid it carefully in the top of the trash can. I hadn't expected the trash man to take it away; I just thought that was a good sort of interim interment. How could I have known the owner was away and I would forget the cat was in the trash can?

Cats don't like us, it's that simple. If you think about those saber tooths and some of the big cats that have managed to make it to modern times, the little household cat has a lot to be ticked about. That little guy who's all curled up in your lap is really thinking about you as hor'dourves: it's just that he's too small to act on it. Somewhere in his past is a five-hundred pound cave lion, a huge tiger, or, at least, a cougar or cheetah. We and our ancestors have gradually starved the little dude until he fits on our lap. If you really knew what meow meant, I suspect you would be scared.

I saw a nature program on television about domestic cats. They followed a bunch of them around for a while and then compared their mannerisms to a bunch of African lions. Well, guess what, the little devils are miniature lions. I'm not kidding. There was this barnyard tomcat that spent most of his day waiting for the female to bring him a mouse our something. In another context, she could have bringing him a wildebeest just like the wilds of Africa. If you'd asked him, he'd tell you there was no difference. It was like watching a horror movie. To think attitudes like that are sleeping on your bed.

Back to the critter at my house: I kept hearing stories about *Sylvia*. Turns out the shelter assigns temporary names to animals in their custody: Sylvia was hers. This cat, I'm sure, was named for Sylvia Plath, the poet, who had a very troubled life. The movie about her had the tagline, *Life was too small to contain her*. Life is too small to contain this Sylvia too. But about this Sylvia there was no end to accolade. What actually was attractive, it turns out, is that the little monster is exactly the same color as our two labs. There the similarity ends. Those two labs are the sweetest creatures that ever walked: the tiny terrorist doesn't have a sweet molecule in her.

Well, it was *Sylvia this and Sylvia that* and how cute she'd be all cuddled up with Sean and Paddy, the two labs. One day the adult leadership came home from the shelter all distraught, *Sylvia was adopted. Yes!* thought I. But the next week

Sylvia was back at the shelter. Now I'm not a brain surgeon, I'm just an old sailor. But even I can figure out that someone who adopts a cat and brings her back a week later has a reason. I was told it was because of allergies. Yeah right, allergic to half-inch deep scratches.

I gave in. Sylvia came home. She was cute looking: has this little smashed in nose, blue eyes. Supposedly she was Himalayan or Nepalese or something: has little orange rings around her tail. She was big time kissing up to the lady of the house. *Oh isn't she sweet.* Well, I stayed clear for a while. I was allowed to name her to soften me up a little. I figured with a Sean and a Paddy and since her birthday was St. Catherine's day, Caitlin was an appropriate name. Actually it's more like a *nom de guerre.*

She immediately started kissing up to the dogs too. Those yellow buffoons never met anything they didn't like: soon they were giving her big sloppy kisses. She didn't seem to mind, not even when a single slurp lifted her six-inches off the floor. But I knew what she was doing. Divide and conquer. Get the adult leadership and the two dogs on her side and I'd find myself sleeping out under the patio table. You could see it in those beady, blue eyes: evil. I kept my distance.

A couple of times, when nobody was looking, I picked her up and tried to stroke her. She's got a set of switchblades that would make a gang member blush. And she's quick too. I lost so much blood I thought I was going to need a transfusion. I was weak for days. I bought her toys. I bought her kitty treats. I said nice things to her. What did she do for me? I'm standing next to the bed with my toes under the dust ruffle while arranging the attire chosen for me by my adult leadership which I intend to wear for the day when the most excruciating pain you can imagine hits my foot. I'm hopping around on one foot cursing the little devil and my adult leadership is yelling at me that I scared her. Scared her! It's a good thing she didn't come in contact with the one foot I had left: talk about catastrophe.

You should see her. I'm sitting at one end of the sofa and she's curled up in my wife's lap. Those eyes are staring at me, daring me. *Ha-ha, you can't touch me because I'm in my mommy's lap.* You can hear that purring, that evil purring. That nature show about the big cats said they purr too. I have this creepy feeling...like I'm a pig-in-a-blanket or something.

Chick Flicks: *A little dated but still apropos*

I visited with my old friend Hogan the other day. Hogan, you probably recall, is now the *concierge* at the Little Bitty Boat Boutique of the Eastern Shore of Maryland. That used to be the Little Bitty Boat Yard: he was the yard boss until the yard owners got uppity. Anyway, Hogan was lamenting the recent crop of movies, particularly the plethora of *chick flicks*. Plethora is my word: his term was *shi*pot load*.

Hogan said his wife had dragged him to see that movie about the amorous cowboys and he wasn't happy about it. I told him I thought that movie was about sheepherders not cowboys. *Whatever*, he said, *it was a chick flick.* He said his wife told him he ought to be more sensitive and accepting. I allowed as how he could probably use a little of both those attributes. I can't repeat here what he said there.

But I certainly agree with him about chick flicks. This weekend my adult leadership and I went to see the movie about the dogs in Antarctica. I have to admit it was a really good movie. But I get tired of getting all sniffily and that was a sniffle generating movie. I long for the days when the cavalry came over the hill or the bad guy made the good guy's day and the universal reaction was a shouted, *Yes!* At the end of those movies your hanky was still in your pocket and you felt just as good as you did when Harry met Sally.

Back in the seventies, movie makers decided action films all had to have a political message. The good guy would be plugging the bad guy with his hand cannon while reminding him that he was being terminated not for some crime but rather his insensitivity toward the nearly extinct, beady-eyed, tush-watcher. I long for the simplicity of good guys and bad guys and *just the facts m'am*.

I marvel at the way computer animation has progressed. Recently, wife and I went to see the *Chronicles of Narnia*, the film adaptation of the wonderful C. S. Lewis books of the same name. I read these books as a kid, read them to my kids, and look forward to reading them to my grandkids. In the movie that lion looked like he was really talking. For someone who grew up with *The Creature From the Black Lagoon* and the Japanese *Godzilla*, I think I can say special effects have come a long way. The *Chronicles of Narnia* had plenty of action but no mayhem. All these mythical creatures were slamming into each other and arrows and spears were flying, rhinos were stomping everything, and giant birds were beaning the bad guys with boulders...yet, amazingly, most everybody remained intact. I think this would strain the credulity of most six-year olds. They see more violence in a *Roadrunner* cartoon. Now, I'm not craving violence. That's not where I'm going here. But if you're going to have violence to further a story line, it ought to be violent. *Narnia* was a chick flick.

Harvard psychologist William Pollack has written much about the struggle modern boys are having being boys. The great movement to make males more sensitive has created problems he proffers. Some of these efforts, Pollack states, can cause so much confusion in the psyche of young men, they can, paradoxically, turn to violence. In other words, shielding young men from violence can cause them to be violent. I'm not saying young men should go out and be violent. But too many chick flicks and not enough where good guys and bad guys duke it out…with the good guy prevailing…might actually be harmful. I have a friend who will not let her small boy-child play with toy guns…so the kid makes a gun with his hand and goes bang-bang anyway.

I think the last really good movie was *Butch Cassidy and the Sundance Kid*. Think about it. This is a movie where the bad guys were really the good guys. That should make those who crave convoluted plots happier than a hog in a waller. There was romance to make those who crave the mushy stuff happy; they blew stuff up; there was catchy music; world travel; and the great Redford was a star. It wasn't a chick flick but you could take a discerning woman to this movie and she felt fulfilled at its conclusion.

I haven't decided yet if all these animated things are chick flicks or not. *Shrek* could have been a chick flick. There were princes and princesses and all that stuff. But there were some really good puns...which one doesn't usually see in a chick flick. Research with puns and women has revealed that when exposed to ten puns to test their appreciation, no pun in ten did. Also none realized that the movie *Love Story* was an allegory about World War III. *Shrek* could have been a much better action movie if somebody had done something to shut that donkey up. Recently, I spent an entire weekend watching and listening to *Ice Age* over and over during a grandkids visit. At first, I thought it was a cute little movie. After about fifty playings however, I started thinking violent thoughts and had to go outside in the snow. I need to rethink that movie.

Used to be comedic movies were sort of gender neutral. Hope and Crosby would do their thing and nobody was made to look too foolish. Among recent movies, I'm still laughing at *Something About Mary* even though the male protagonist was badly abused. You would have to see it to know what I mean. Come to think of it, several of the recent comedies have kind of played upon our weaknesses as men: our tendency to fall in love with beautiful women, eat to excess, fondness for fast cars, like that. *Wedding Crashers*, much of it filmed near our home and in which a number of friends were extras, exploited men terribly. It was chock full of conniving women who played upon men's weaknesses. That's a chick flick of the worst kind.

I want John Wayne to come back. He was always the good guy. He was chivalrous and the ladies appreciated it. He had tremendous courage. You always knew he was going to win so you could leave the theater for a few minutes to take care of some business and know when you got back, John had persevered. There were beautiful ladies and romance too but John knew how to deal with it. Anything that progressed beyond a kiss to the back of the hand was only implied. In the old days, the good guys went after bad guys and engaged in heated battle: today the actors are just in heat. But the chick's like it.

So I told my good friend Hogan to just calm down. I told him I doubt we will ever see the old kinds of movies again. Too many women are buying tickets to movies these days and the movie makers know a market when they see it. So we will have to be happy with animated automobiles and toy soldiers to fill in for John Wayne and Butch Cassidy and his friend. Hogan sort of sighed and said he agreed with me. *The worst part*, he said, *is that movie about the sheepherders: I will never look at Tonto and The Lone Ranger the same again.*

Cliché...No Way: *I'm a sucker for big brown eyes*

There was a time when things looked bleak. A relationship I had vowed would endure forever hadn't. I lived alone and suppressed my unhappiness by working too hard. I planned to buy a boat and live aboard it, so I bought a house. Made sense at the time.

One day, in spite of feeling pretty sorry, I had an inspiration: I called the animal shelter. I made a simple request: please put my name on whatever list they maintained for specific kinds of dogs. I wanted a female lab puppy. I asked the nice lady to please call me if one turned up. To my amazement she said come see them, they had a beautiful female lab puppy.

I had been thinking about a dog for some time: thought perhaps having one would kinda cheer things up a bit. I had remodeled the house, creating for myself my ideal apartment in the walk-in basement. I figured it might be ideal for a pooch too.

Dogs have always been part of my life. My grandfather trained pointers. I helped him train them and hunted behind them as a kid. My family had pet dogs, usually of indeterminate linage, beloved, tick-bitten and flea infested. As an adult there had always been a hound around, some small furry thing that appealed to whatever woman I was married to at the time. I wanted a lab but never prevailed.

This time it was going to be my dog. I aimed my rickety old jeep in the direction of the shelter and milked as much speed out of it as I dared. I don't even remember the trip. I was ecstatic. I remember clearly holding her in my arms the first time. She was gorgeous: big, inquisitive eyes; black, wet nose; and velvet ears. Her black puppy fur was soft as down. Her pink tongue was slobbery and quick. I had kisses all over my face before I could even say hello. Her name came to me as I held her that first time: I introduced myself to Molly.

I wanted to take her home right then but the rules forbade it. I had to be *approved*. During the next week a person from the shelter came to my home and inspected it and interviewed me. The house and I passed. Molly could come home and we could begin our life together. As soon as I got the thumbs up, I ordered L.L. Bean's best cedar filled dog bed.

I don't remember the first Labrador retriever I met. They have always just been there: blond, black, and chocolate. I guess some friend or colleague must have had one, I just don't remember. They weren't particularly popular in Florida when I was growing up. I suppose that was because labs are happier in cooler climes. Somewhere along the way they must have adapted, I see them in bunches now when I go back to visit.

Today, labs are the most popular breed in America according to the American Kennel Club. I don't doubt that. My Molly is the sweetest animal that ever poked along on footpads. And the thousands of her brothers and sisters I see here on the Eastern Shore of Maryland must have similar dispositions. Nothing else that I can think of would explain that much popularity. To be sure, labs are great hunting dogs but I don't think that's why nearly every station wagon or pickup truck on this side of the Chesapeake Bay has one for a co-pilot.

The Waterfowl Festival is a big shindig in Easton, Maryland and my wife and I usually volunteer. Part of the festival is the retriever trials. Last year a friend suggested we go to the trials and watch the dogs. What an incredible experience. The labs weren't the only retrievers participating but they were the ones I was interested in. It is amazing to see the sheer joy these animals experience when they go after the stuffed duck or whatever that thing was they retrieved. When they worked their way back to their handler, wagging and dripping, they were beside themselves with happiness. When they looked into their handler's eyes you could imagine them saying, *See what a good dog I am? I did this just for you.* Amazing!

My Molly could never hunt. Molly is the only lab I have ever known that does not like to swim: she will but she doesn't like it. When I throw her stick into the water she goes but I get this look that says, *I'll do this for you but don't think for a minute that I enjoy it.* Her hips are a little stiff and the vet says swimming is good for her so we exercise with the stick in the water but I know she goes after it as an act of love. And you can forget shotguns too. Molly cringes when she hears the starting gun for the sailboat races—a quarter of a mile away.

Molly is twelve now and has slowed. She has a little gray in her muzzle and a little stiffness in her hips. Her bark has changed. She has a minor paralysis in her vocal cords—just something we have to watch. She sounds like a seal and we laugh. It just makes her wag that much harder. But her life has taken a serious turn and she is not happy about it. Paddy came to live with us. Paddy, a yellow lab puppy, arrived at our home just last week.

Molly has had a procession of granddogs visit over the years and generally accepts them, plays with a few, and ignores the others. Somehow she knew this one wasn't going home. Her patented look of disdain, the one she gives me when I throw the stick in the water, has become commonplace. *Dad, why did you do this to me?*

When Molly and I married Susie, a blond cocker spaniel came with the deal. Buttercup didn't like Molly any more than Molly likes Paddy. But over time they became sisters. When Buttercup became terminally ill, we had to make that awful decision. Molly was sad for weeks and would hardly eat. Dogs do that. Eventually she perked up but you knew something was missing from her life.

I think she will accept Paddy soon. How could she not love that little fluffy yellow thing? But right now she is not pleased. It is fun to watch her compensate. Paddy has no compunctions about the water. He leaps in and revels in the wonder of it, splashing and jumping and just savoring the sheer joy of being wet. Molly says, *Okay, if this is what I have to do to get this kid to go home, I'll act like I like it too.* And she bounces in after him. But keeps her distance.

When Molly finally accepts Paddy, we hope he will learn from her. She is a peaceful, well-mannered, pleasing animal. She loves unabashedly. If that little guy picks up some of those traits we will be very happy. As much as we wish it weren't true, Molly won't be around forever. And we know the time will come when we have to make that awful decision again. That little bouncy blond ball of fluff will be a good way to have part of her with us for another few years.

An overly sophisticated friend of mine asked why we got another lab, *Labs are such a cliché.* How can anyone feel that way about an animal that has so much love to give? Cliché…no way!

Note: We lost Molly soon after this piece was written.

Goodbye Molly: *Some of this you've heard before; she was special*

I suppose it's normal on the eve of a new year to look back and think about things. My wife and I called 2003 *the year from hell*. It seems we spent the whole year mourning. We lost a parent, a sister, 3 neighbors, a kitty and our sweet Molly. It is never easy to lose family and friends: we continue to grieve for them. But Molly was special and I miss her in a special way: she was my *baby dog*.

Molly was only about eight-weeks old when I first met her. I say about because I got her from the animal shelter and they didn't know her exact age. They weren't even sure what breed she was though it was pretty clear she was mostly black lab. She had a coal black nose and little velvety floppy ears that she cocked back when she was curious. When I held her the first time and got a great big wet kiss I knew we belonged together.

I grew up in a family that considered dogs expendable. We had a bunch of them and I'm embarrassed now when I think about how poorly they were treated. We weren't mean to them; they just lived outside and were fed table scraps. My grandfather raised and trained hunting dogs. Those animals were treated far better than the poor mutts at our house but it was strictly hands off. I remember those creatures pulling on their chains trying to get someone to pat their heads and say something nice to them.

When I had children of my own, animals were part of the family. My children, grown now, love animals and respect them and that makes me proud. But those animals were family animals. I never owned a dog that was all mine...until Molly.

Because Molly was a shelter dog I had to go through the wickets. My house and yard were inspected and shelter representatives interviewed me. I passed their tests and Molly moved in. She immediately began training me. She did all the puppy things and we learned together what her needs were and how I was to behave. When she needed to go out, I stopped what I was doing and out she went. She never barked: she just had this look. Molly had a repertoire of looks and everyone who knew her soon learned them.

In those days, my prime mover was an old Jeep Wrangler. Molly rode in the right-hand seat. That was her seat. She had this regal look when she was seated beside me. Once when I was entering a military base, the guard, seeing Molly in the right hand seat, said, *The animal has to ride in back*. He was an idiot. She gave him a look that said as much and she climbed into the rear. As soon as we got off base she climbed back into her seat. I think she looked over her shoulder at the guard. Probably good she couldn't talk.

Molly and I would to go to the local park and play tennis ball. She would play ball until she dropped...or I did. It mattered not how far I threw the ball, she would find it and come back like a rocket. I would hold out my hand and she would drop it in, always very gently. Then she would tremble until I threw it again.

Water was not her thing. The park where we played ball had a nice stream full of rocks. It was shallow and the banks sloped down to sandy edges. I would walk down the middle of the stream, wading or stepping rock to rock and Molly would walk along the edge. She wouldn't even touch the water if she could avoid it. If I crossed to the other side, she would stand on the opposite bank and cry until I came and got her. Eventually she learned to swim but it never pleased her. I would throw a stick or ball in the water and she would reluctantly go after it giving me the same look of contempt she gave that gate guard when she was a puppy.

Molly and I got married and she was very happy with her new family. There was a cocker spaniel named Buttercup who quickly became her sister and mentor. Buttercup taught Molly to go over the fence and go exploring. They were *known* to the pound. They made a cute pair: little blond cocker and big black lab. When Buttercup died, Molly mourned. It was quite a while before she got her spirit back.

We moved to the Eastern Shore of Maryland and Molly was pretty happy about the idea. There were lots of other dogs to play with and she had plenty of places to go fetch things. She always learned tricks easily and was pretty charming in her own way. She balanced the cookie on her nose and then snapped it up, seldom missing. She would roll over on command but sometimes got locked into the trick and kept rolling until someone physically stopped her. She had so many fans she won first place in the local dog show. Her little trophy is still prominent in our family room.

When she was twelve, her new brother came to live with us. He was a cute little blond guy. My wife and I knew we wouldn't have Molly forever and hoped she would help us train him. We got that look of pure disdain many times in those first few weeks after Paddy moved in. Paddy was a good dog too and I think, in part, Molly is responsible.

Molly developed a paralysis of her vocal chords. At first we teased her because her bark sounded like a seal. The vet said this condition often happens with labs and she would probably be okay. This summer, when the weather was hot, she was not okay. She had trouble breathing and couldn't go for walks anymore. When we left for walks, she would stand by the door with a pitiful look: she just didn't understand what was wrong with her. She still loved to play ball but just couldn't do it. We knew the time was coming but it was hard to talk about. One night she paced all night long. She was in pain and was suffering. My baby dog looked at me with a special look and I knew I had to take her on that last ride in the right hand seat. I lifted her in and as I drove stroked her head and ears all the way to the vet's. I couldn't stay for the final event; I'm not that brave. I will never forget the look she gave me as I walked away. I will forever regret that I didn't stay by her side. Goodbye Molly, I will always love you.

Confessions of a Mullet Eater: *And to heck with fish snobs*

People who hail from my bend in the creek eat a fish called mullet. I eat mullet. Got that? I'm a mulletavore. If you're from the Panhandle of Florida where I was raised, you probably eat mullet too. I won't do a *Bubba Gump* on you and list all the ways you can prepare mullet: there are plenty. Smoked, broiled, or fried is customary: all those other ways are just highfalutin. Except for eating the roe, the eggs of the mullet, which is not highfalutin because no person who faluted highly would ever eat mullet roe. Common folk in North Florida, among whom I profess fealty, eat mullet roe for breakfast.

Now why did I bring this up? I've been pestered by some people who do not know from mullet: they are piscisnobs, from the Latin *piscis* meaning fish and snob meaning snob. Piscisnobs look down on mullet…and mullet eaters. When pressed, piscisnobs will confess total ignorance regarding the gustatory perfection of fried mullet choosing to base their prejudice on the eating habits of the mullet, a very poor argument.

To be sure, a mullet's appetite, if given much thought, could affect one's own appetite. They eat detritus. That's a great word *detritus*. If you open your Funk and Wagnall's, you'll discover detritus is: *organic debris left after the decomposition of plants and animals*. That means detritus is in the same family as that stuff which gets flushed. To the average mullet, detritus is haute cuisine. The mullet processes the useful parts of detritus and the rest becomes, well, detritus. One of the characteristics of the mullet is its manner of dining: moving along the bottom at a forty-five degree angle, like a little finny vacuum, suctioning goodies from the mud. When eating mullet, you best not think of its diet.

I want to get back to that snob thing. I'd like to point out that while criticizing the poor mullet's choice of lunch, the piscisnobs think nothing of a crab's menu. Mullet are downright fastidious when you compare their dining habits with those of crabs. Piscisnobs not only pick crabs, they slurp oysters. I'm told by people smarter and better educated than me that part of the problem with Chesapeake Bay is too few oysters. Why? Because oysters are filters. What do they filter? Yep. Somebody flushes their detritus up in New York

State and down the Susquehanna it comes. Oysters in Chesapeake Bay try to clean it up. Of course a lot of the oysters get sick and die, but they die trying. If you've ever eaten an oyster that tastes a little like a Coney Island hotdog, now you know why. So next time you think about what a mullet eats piscisnob, have another oyster or pick another crab.

I have to admit that the word mullet itself is kind of inelegant. Of course fish names in general are kind of lacking: rock fish, croaker, crappie. See what I mean? Back in 1965 there was an effort in Florida to change the name of the humble mullet to something more elegant: Lisa. Apparently fish named Lisa didn't go over very well: mullet it remains.

Folks from my part of the world are just plain folks. North Florida is the southern part of the state…you'll figure that out. Of course there's been an invasion so that seems to be changing a bit but folks still have a lot of southern charm and gentility. You might find some fancy food on the menu of an old fashioned fish house in north Florida but that just reflects that gentility previously mentioned. Hospitality dictates that you provide food for guests that they deem palatable. But for the home folk there will be fried mullet and hushpuppies and sweet iced tea.

The Panhandle of Florida is mostly sand. Except in the fertile river bottoms, about the only thing that grows well are pine trees and rattlesnakes. In my youth, the common folk mostly worked in the pulpwood business or fished for mullet. The tree wranglers and mullet fishermen I knew were hard working, hard playing, responsible folks of strong faith and values. Mullet fishermen and tree wranglers are descendants of the original crackers. Crackers were the oxen and mule skinners who drove animals pulling sledges of timber across the sands of Georgia, Alabama and Florida in the olden days, their sobriquet derived from the crack of their whips. Cracker is not a derisive term where I grew up.

So to you piscisnobs out there who've never enjoyed mullet, the loss is yours. Enjoy your own bottom feeders and leave the mullet to us crackers. We're right happy with our lot and will lift a glass of tea to you regardless of your prejudice. By the way, North Florida crabs and oysters are good too.

For Your Tomorrow: *In which I get a little serious*

In the spring of 1944 the Japanese advance into India was halted by soldiers of the British Empire at the small town of Kohima in the northeast corner of that country. The fighting was intense and bloody. At a cemetery in Kohima where soldiers of the British Empire are buried, a bronze plaque reads, *When you go home, tell them of us and say, for your tomorrow, we gave our today.*

Recently I had a conversation with a good friend who had just returned from the Middle East. His stories were very familiar to me, reflections my own experiences almost 50 years ago in Southeast Asia. My friend left a piece of his soul in those tormented sands: I'm still haunted by shadows of the Vietnam jungles. When we come home, we try to put the memories of war behind us and resume a normal life...but the shadows are always there, they never go away. The smell of grilled steak can resurrect awful images; fireworks on the Fourth of July remind one of rockets and mortars that were not festive; the beat of rotors on a passing helicopter; burning trash; guns in the distance during hunting season...sounds and images that pry apart our tranquility with the finesse of a wrecking bar.

Most of us who've experienced the horrific things that come with war return to loving families who help us push the images back into the recesses. Most of us were healthy before the experiences and have a before to mitigate the after. Some, deeply scarred by their experiences, came home to situations with which they cannot cope. But all of us gave part of our tomorrows in those days when we saw, touched, smelled, and heard the horrors of battle.

Not long ago newspapers carried stories about a study involving soldiers in Afghanistan and Iraq. The study seemed to imply our soldiers have suffered significant ethical decline. Questions were asked of the soldiers regarding their willingness to ignore acts by their peers against civilians. I was appalled, not by the responses which seemed to imply some would look the other way, but by the audacity of someone asking a teenager, in a combat zone, a hypothetical question such as that. I'm not amazed at all that the troops responded the way they did. In a combat zone the world is turned upside down, a *Wonderland* world that Lewis Carroll would clearly understand. Ask a kid in high school would he rat on a friend. He'd say no, but yet would if the situation warranted. Put him in a school where people are dying all around and his life depends on that friend. His *today* is significantly impacted by the circumstances. In response to a hypothetical question, he has an easy answer. But, based on my own experience, he would do the right thing. Some would not…but the kid who was healthy and came from a good home, circumstances which define most American service people, would.

The same articles implied the incidence of Post-Traumatic Stress Disorder has grown. I doubt that. We're probably just better at identifying a malady that's been around forever: shell shock, battle fatigue, whatever.

Memorial Day is special to me. This is a day to remember those who gave their todays for your tomorrows. This is a day to remember those whose tomorrows were forever altered because they were willing to give their today for your tomorrow. Memorial Day is not a day for pity. No one of healthy mind wants pity. Memorial Day is a day for respect. Respect is often not asking a question. Yes, war is tough. Yes, most that experience battle have memories they would rather not share with you…unless, of course, you've been there too. They choose not to share not because of disrespect for you…but, because you cannot understand. If you weren't there then you cannot understand. No, it's not like *Saving Private Ryan*. No, it's not like *Full Metal Jacket* or *Hacksaw Ridge*. No, it's not like movies starring John Wayne and James Stewart. They don't want to answer your questions about personal experiences in combat. If you'd been there yourself, you would never ask those questions. They would like for you to honor their experience and, most of all, remember those friends who didn't come back the way they went over. That's what Memorial Day means to a healthy veteran.

I am a student of military history: have been since I was a kid. One thing I believe to be true based on my experience and reading: you cannot survive in war if you don't believe. Beliefs vary, to be sure, but belief in one's self, one's mates, one's family, one's country, one's faith…those are the beliefs that get you through and get you home. It is sad that much of what we read focuses on the experiences of those whose beliefs are impaired…they commit atrocities, abuse prisoners, lie, cheat, steal. But those whose beliefs are sound, they are willing to give their today for your tomorrow. Respect them on Memorial Day.

Behold the Mighty Hunter: *My elephant gun is my computer mouse*

I am the mighty hunter: my mouse is my bow, my cursor my arrow and Google my quiver. I can target anything and with the click of my left button, slinging my arrow zinging on its path. I don't need a safari-suit, native bearers or background noises of obnoxious jungle sounds. I can hunt in my skivvies if it suits me and my prey is every bit as vulnerable as Lord Whomever's as he skulks about the mighty jungle in search of elusive prey.

Those of you who have read my meanderings know of my antipathy for the decidedly feminine pastime *shopping*. Detest it. Can't tolerate it. I'd rather gargle with broken glass. Yuck! I'm told this is a normal condition of those of us who swizzle testosterone in our veins. We share a dislike for pondering endlessly the nuances of certain items of apparel, et cetera. Well, if indeed you and I are of like mind, consider the value of the Internet. You can stalk your quarry in a most expeditious manner and with only a few clicks your prey is on its way to you at whatever speed you choose to fund.

Most of my life I've considered shopping a warlike activity. More than a few times I've sat in my conveyance considering appropriate tactics for marching into the fray, grabbing my whatever and clearing the obstacles in the least possible time. *Once more into the breach my friends… .* Shakespeare knew; *Hank V* knew. I would sit there and watch the ebb and flow through the doors of the targeted mercantile establishment, pondering the order of battle. Forty-eleven-dozen snotty nosed kids and their tattooed mothers in, ten out. Fifty obese, work-release dudes in sweaty muscle-shirts in, none out. Twenty swanky ladies in, only a few out. Formidable opposition.

But into the breach I must go. I cross the threshold, dodging, bobbing, weaving, grabbing off the shelf, and then retreat. The last obstacle, other than the lady who makes sure you're not trying to sneak some purloined something out of the place, is the checkout. Other than actually entering the establishment, the checkout is my least favorite experience. I always seem to be in line behind the checkout clerk's very best friend. They talk about the babies, the most recent peccadilloes of acquaintances and how the cost of disposable diapers seems to be going nowhere but up. They are oblivious to others in the line. I try to interest myself in the latest cookbook for crock-pot dinners or who, this week, is having an affair with some actress or actor whose name I don't even recognize or if Princess Diana's wreck was caused by aliens. Then there's the checkout line chatter.

Some checkout line conversation cannot be ignored: you're not eavesdropping, it's unavoidable. I'm sure I stand there with my mouth agape. Some would make my old navy buddies blush.

When stores started installing the self-checkout lanes, I was heartened. Tactically, I knew I could go in harm's way, grab my whatever and go directly to the self-checkout. With practice I reduced my in-store time considerably. And then the opposition discovered self-checkout. And what's worse, there seems to be no self-checkout etiquette. Not that there's much etiquette in the normal checkout but usually there's a functional queue. Not so in self-checkout. You're waiting for a little old lady to scan the last of her cartload when, just as she retrieves her receipt, out of nowhere comes one of those fat dudes in the muscle shirt, sneering around his toothpick and hugging to his jiggling chest 20 cans of motor oil. You think I'm going to tell him he's jumped the line? My momma didn't raise no fool. So much for a good idea: back to pondering tactics in the parking lot.

At first I was very reluctant to shop on the Internet. When you plug in those plastic numbers, who the heck knows where they're going. But after a few successes it was easier...but I was still cautious. I checked all the reviews and comments.

It there was any question at all, I clicked on the next Google hit. To date, I've only had one bad experience and that was resolved to my satisfaction.

A nice thing about Internet shopping is the reviews. You can do a simple search for *best value* and get amazing information about both merchants and merchandise. A couple of Christmases ago, I bought my better half a digital camera. I quickly encountered some *bait and switch* operations. There were several engaging in this nefarious practice. I quickly added comments about the dealers I caught doing this dirty deed to the *Epinions* website. I don't know if that stopped them but I certainly felt like I'd done a good deed. *Epinions* is worth a look if you haven't visited them before.

I've done a lot of business on eBay. It was on eBay that I had my one bad experience. They rectified the situation very quickly and banned a dealer from further business. I even bought a vehicle on eBay and have been very satisfied with the result. I've heard of others who weren't happy…so *caveat emptor*.

Sitting at my desk doing business is infinitely more satisfying that banging around in some store with the inconsiderate masses. I can search for the best deal, find things I'd have to go to the big city for (an experience ranking only slightly below shopping in terms of dissatisfaction for me), get ideas for gifts, and, actually, enjoy a bit of that evil experience…shopping. I can get reviews of products that I need or think I need. I can find manuals for things I bought and threw the manuals away. I can actually buy presents for my adult leadership without her guidance.

When I'm after something, I Google, select, pay and be done with it. I get this sense of satisfaction. A couple of days later I receive on my doorstep whatever it was I needed. I know what the ancient hunters felt. Killing things never made me very happy so I've never experienced the reward some get for this activity. To me, securing a cartridge for my inkjet printer at a good price and finding the sucker on my doorstep a few days later must be akin to the feelings some have when they blast a goose out of the air. And my sport is a whole lot less messy.

So, I'm stalking the elusive willow-winged widget. There it is nestled between pop-ups for male enhancement potions and software for inventorying wombats. Quickly my cursor zeros in. With a swift movement of my left mouse-key I nail the sucker. A couple of clicks later my willow-winged widget is paid for, packaged and en route to my doorstep. With the provided shipping code I can track its every movement from source to destination. I smile. I'm the mighty hunter.

Confessions of a Curmudgeon: *My adult leadership broke the code*

Alas, Andy Rooney has passed. My heart is broken. My role-model is gone. In early October of 2011, Rooney left to provide commentary in heaven. One can only imagine the topics upon which he will rant: Pearly Gates are too extravagant; the golden streets get slippery in the clouds; all that lyre music gets tiresome; angel feathers everywhere (Why do angels have to molt anyway?). I'm sure he'll find ample subject matter.

Being a curmudgeon is not a bad thing. We curmudgeons give everyone pause...make you think about things. You don't have to agree, just think about it. Before you're old enough to warrant the curmudgeon sobriquet, you had pet peeves. When you get older, you're just grouchy...curmudgeonly. Rooney and I shared a lot of opinions. I'm told he did over 1,500 essays during his minute or so on the program *60 Minutes*. That's a bit more peevish than I think I am but we still have many issues in common.

One issue Andy and I shared was our opinions of shopping carts...neither of us like them. We both agree that the height of laziness is the person who just leaves their shopping cart in the parking lot for someone else to return to the store or cart corral. That really frosts my cookies. And, inevitably, the parking place that I've decided is the best in the lot, has a cart squarely in the middle of it. I have to get out of the car, move the cart, park the car, and then, griping the whole way, return it. I think people who leave their carts in the parking places should have an extra tax on their Wheaties, or maybe they could be denied access to those sanitizer wipes at the store entrance. Then they would get a horrible case of the flu or the green difugus…they deserve it.

While we're on the topic of shopping carts, somebody tell me why Walmart buys carts with square wheels. Have you ever noticed that? It's bad enough trying to navigate up and down the overly congested aisles avoiding other square wheeled carts but that thunk-thunk noise will make you hate your mother. Walmart has this nifty little electric cart pusher that allows a bazillion carts to be moved from the corrals to the store. Ever had to wait before backing out while one of those cart-trains moved past? Makes you wish you'd packed a lunch. Ever been there?

On the subject of shopping, whoever designed those *self-checkout* systems in stores, obviously never used one. Those things make the scrutiny of the *Patriot Act* seem no worse than the neighborhood busybody, to wit: *The weight of the item on the belt is not the same as the item scanned, please wait for assistance.* So I do…and the head of the 3 person queue at the register I avoided by using the self-checkout waves as he goes out the door…and I'm still waiting for assistance. I buy lots of yoghurt, a dozen or so cups at a whack. Each one has to be scanned at the self-checkout. And don't ever buy a bottle of wine in that fashion. The powers are convinced you're an underage teenager in a wrinkled birthday suit. The local Walmart got rid of self-checkout…too much pilferage. Probably by people who got fed up and walked out.

I'll give shopping a rest for a moment. Let's consider rude drivers. People who go beyond the stop-line at intersections astonish me. For the in-cognoscenti among us and those still peddling velocipedes, the stop-line is that broad, usually white, line back of which you are supposed to stop at stop signs or traffic signals. When you go beyond it, people turning towards you must swing widely to get around. Big trucks have a particularly difficult time with this maneuver. People who do this should be strapped to the front of a car stopped 10 feet in front of the stop line...and then let a few big trucks go by. That'll be some close brushes. It's rude to do this: don't. I feel better.

Andy Rooney had this curmudgeon stuff mastered. He should have: he was still griping at age 92. I probably won't make that. I'll probably get run over by a train of square wheeled shopping carts stopped in front of the stop-line at Walmart: thunk-thunk-oops. I do think age contributes to curmudgeoness. When you've got fewer minutes left than you've already expended, things with which you've been patient all those years become irritants. And, since you're of the age when nobody listens to you anyway, you might as well spout off. I'm not sure anyone actually listened to Andy Rooney. I think they just wanted to see what ticked him off most recently.

My adult leadership, who always stops in front of the stop-line, has perfected the art of

ignoring me. That's okay, you still listen to me.
You do don't you?

Cars and Such Truck: *A multi-cylinder symphony*

To say that I'm a car enthusiast would be an understatement. My first memories involve a car, actually a jeep. My earliest days were spent on the campus of Florida State University where my father was enrolled. Married student housing was in an area called *West Campus*, in buildings that had been part of an WWII Army Air Force Base. Intermingled with married student housing were fraternity houses. Florida State had morphed in 1947, the year following the year of my nativity, from the Florida State College for Women…an occurrence the University of Florida continues to suggest influences its cousins' mastery of field sports. Most of the fraternity brethren in my neighborhood were novitiates and veterans of the recently ended world conflict. They were nice. They had great fun teasing a four year-old who tried as often as he could to go visit them on his tricycle. One of them owned a jeep. It was green with bright yellow wheels. I was the four year-old and I fell in love with that jeep.

I am plagued with memory. I've been told it's unusual to remember things that occur when one's four years-old. I remember lots of things that happened when I was four and maybe even earlier. Clogs my memory and limits what I can absorb now at my advanced age. Never mind that, I remember that jeep and I remember the owner saying I could have it if I could start it. He must have thought I was a dumb little four year-old because I knew you had to have a key and he wouldn't give it to me. I remember that. Been fretting about that frat ever sense. I sure loved that jeep.

The jeep was the first car with which I fell in love and the beginning of an affair that continues yet. In actual fact, there has never been a car that I didn't like. I can see something in all of them. The first car I owned was not a car at all. It was a Ford Model-A truck. It had started its life as a sedan and somewhere along the way had an encounter with metal shears and a gas torch. I paid a friend of my father's ten-dollars for it. I took it apart and put it back together many times. It never ran and I couldn't find an adult with any mechanical prowess or inclination to play mechanic with a kid, so it just lived on the edge of the woods back of my house, its tires flat and an assortment of its parts spread out on the oil stained plywood that served as its pickup bed. But I sure had fun disassembling and reassembling it. While I was visiting with my grandparents for a couple of weeks, my mother gave it away. Broke my heart.

As a kid who loved tinkering with cars, I think I may have lived in Eden. There were junk yards ripe for the picking and junk-yard owners who were generous with kids. I paid a quarter for a carburetor once, a Stromberg 97 off an old race car (flathead Ford V8): it had six Strombergs. I didn't have an engine on which to put it, I just wanted to own a Stromberg 97. Wish I still had it. I think my mother gave that away too. Over the years things have gotten better. I've owned clapped-out old Chevies and top-of-the-line Porsches and a few *family flivvers* too. All in all, I haven't been deprived.

I inherited an old 1949 Chevy from my grandfather (by way of my older brother). I rebuilt the transmission, engine, and brakes on that old clunker. Actually, I replaced the transmission with one from a 1938 Chevy that belonged to my girlfriend's father. My girlfriend's father continues to reside in my list of heroes: he was a machinist and fabricated a new drive shaft for the Chevy, the original being a contrivance called a *torque tube*. Mr. Folsom was an adult who would take time with a kid. He taught me much about mechanics. From him I learned one of the best lessons in life, *Buy at least one more of a given item than you think you'll need. If you buy an extra, you're likely not to need it: if you don't you will.* That particular lesson had to do with piston rings for those of you among the cognoscenti. I think of that lesson every time I go to a hardware store.

I owned a 1962, Porsche 356B, for 17 years: miss that car. I took it to Germany with me when I was stationed there. There was nothing on that car that I couldn't repair. I raced gymkhana with it before gymkhana became autocross. I was good too. I loved that little car. It had a perpetual problem with rust and I think I invested a small fortune in my battle against oxygen but that was the only major difugalty. I sold it before I moved to the Eastern Shore of Maryland, in essence declaring defeat in the rust wars. Considering the salt-laden air in which we live, it was probably a wise move. That little *bathtub Porsche* was a pretty thing: *signal red* with a factory sunroof.

I once worked with a mechanic who was illiterate. He couldn't even write his name. But he was one of the smartest people I've ever known. He used test instruments, complicated test instruments in his day, with no difficulty. He just couldn't read or write. Today, he'd probably be identified as one who suffered from a learning disability. Back in the early sixties you didn't hear much about dyslexia and such. His name was Buck and I learned a bunch from him. He taught me to listen. A running engine is a symphony. There are bass notes and tinny, high notes and rhythmic nuances; enough to impress any discerning symphonic conductor. Every one of those notes says something about a running engine. Buck would stand there with his hand on his chin just experiencing the sounds. Then he would identify the malady and fix it. You think you could diagnose an engine today by listening to it? You can't even tell if it's running. I suspect old Buck is upstairs tuning up God's golf cart, but I'll bet he would shake his head at today's diagnostic equipment. Diagnosis codes indeed. I thought Buck was one of a kind with his special ear but I've now met another: my daughter –in-law's father Keith, also a master mechanic, has an ear like that. I have benefitted.

Over the years I've owned and raced cars and driven cars owned by others, road racing and autocross, but mostly I've just enjoyed working on them. To me there is great satisfaction in working on a car...or a truck. When everything is put together and you turn that key, there's this moment when you wonder. Sometimes it's frustrating, often a delight. Sometimes you run a little short of skill and talent and you have to seek an expert. In my village we have a master mechanic. Stacy is another of those very patient people who graciously explains problems. I know he must think I'm an idiot with some of the questions I've asked but he's never shown that he does. I'm grateful. I still *bend a wrench* on a couple of old vehicles, I still get satisfaction from it.

Our family conveyance is one of those ubiquitous Swedish station wagons that are touted to stand up to a collision with anything short of an Abrams tank. I can't repair squat on it. I can't even change a light bulb. I've never noticed if Swedish people have small hands but they must. Either that or they've got a troop of trained four year-olds. I don't even know where the spark plugs are on this car: sure as heck can't see anything that looks like a spark plug. Makes me wonder: what do kids today wrench on if they want to learn automobile mechanics? When I was a kid, you didn't need much more than a Crescent wrench and a ballpeen hammer to do most automobile repairs. Today the list of *special tools* fills a two-inch deep, three-ring binder... or a gigabyte of computer memory. Special tools indeed! And you better be a computer wizard if you want to be a mechanic. Our rearview mirror died. Good question, *How does a rearview mirror die*? Turns out it's a *liquid crystal display*. Cost six-hundred bucks to replace. I didn't. Can't go to the junk yard anymore, even if you could find one, and pay five-bucks for one off a wreck.

My adult leadership could do without my wrenching. I'm not like some of today's mechanics who wear surgical gloves when they work. When I come home from working on my thirty year-old jeep ambulance, I'm covered in grease and usually have blood oozing from my knuckles. I smell like an old-fashioned garage. She makes me strip off my dirty clothes and head for the shower, visually demonstrating her distaste for my smell and appearance. That's okay. I'm tired and the shower feels good. And it gives me a few moments to reflect on how satisfying it is to turn that key and hear that symphony.

Ken Doll? *Not really*

I suspect everybody knows Ken. Certainly everybody knows Barbie, at least anyone who has daughters or granddaughters: Ken was Barbie's beau. I'm told he was replaced...know that feeling well...with a dude named Blaine but supposedly he's making a comeback. I always felt real sorry for Ken. It's probably good he got dumped by Barbie. If I were asked for advice, I'd tell him to go find another plastic chick. In my experience, there's an abundance of plastic chicks. Barbie's got this pinched waist that will, undoubtedly, lead to bowel problems in her later years. I see lots of medical bills and a bit of inconvenience. That cute little posterior already shows some signs of disproportionate growth: spa bills. And that hair: she'll never be happy when that goes gray. I think Ken would do better elsewhere since he's been given a choice.

By now you're wondering where I'm going with this aren't you? Well, I've decided that some women never got over Ken. It's just a theory but I think it has merit. Some women, even in their grandmother years, are still trying to dress Ken. I thought I'd call that *Ken Doll Syndrome* but that moniker has already been captured (I *Googled* it.). It relates to women who've had a *tummy-tuck* and afterwards feel as though they're, uh, *equipped*.

I'm not making this up. So that title was out. But still, it is sort of a syndrome, women feeling as though they have to dress up the man (men, boys) in their life as though they were Ken dolls. We have that problem in our house: the clothes thing, not the other.

My mother had a theory about pickup trucks. She was the mother of five boys so she probably had a good statistical population from which to work. She theorized that boys who didn't get enough time with their little red wagons as children would naturally gravitate towards pickup trucks. Now, as I recall, there was always an abundance of red wagons around our house so that may, in fact, not be the reason all her sons have pickup trucks but it's a nice theory. My sister went the Barbie and Ken route. I'm sure if you could get sociologists to agree on anything, they would say that the deprivations we all suffer as children influence our adult lives. I've never had the nerve to ask my adult leadership if she was deprived of clothes for her Ken dolls but there is some evidence.

As most of you know, I spent a few years in the navy: thirty-one years actually. Every working day I got up, cleaned up, and put on a uniform. And that uniform had to be perfect. It was sort of a *thing* with me. Shoes had to be perfect. Brass had to be polished. Cover (hat) had to be just so. After thirty-one years, I was a little tired of that. I looked forward to the days when I could wear a knit shirt and khaki pants: socks optional. I feel like I kind of earned that privilege. I live fairly close to one of those outlet-malls. It's great. I can nip in there and grab a knit shirt or two, go by the shoe outlet for some new boat shoes, whip over the L. L. Bean's for some britches and be done in forty-five minutes…flat. I guess you could argue that I've replaced one uniform with another and that's fine with me…I choose the uniform I wear now. Except for when I get overruled.

I should have realized in those days of wonder and awe when I first met my wife that she was going to try and dress me. I thought it was kind of sweet when she bought me a sports jacket from a place I couldn't afford to even enter. And then got me a shirt that wasn't one bit better than the one I got at the discount store, just ten-times the price. But she smiled and said she loved me and wanted me to have nice things. That's a really nice sentiment. And her tastes were…and are…impeccable. I tried to tell her about my philosophy that if L. L. Bean didn't sell it, I didn't need it. She wasn't familiar with L. L. Bean.

I have to admit that I cut a dashing figure in my navy uniforms. Literally thousands of women had commented on how dashing I was. Maybe a bit fewer but still a lot. Even when all my hair fell out and my tummy started to show the effects of entirely too much pizza. I think I reminded them of famous naval figures from history. Many of them lacked thatch and sported a bit of a tubby tummy. Never mind all that, my wife thought I looked pretty good too and that's what counted. So as long as I was the dashing naval figure, I didn't get all those *gifts* except on birthdays and holidays. She must have been really frustrated.

When I retired and entered the private sector, wife and I went to a famous discount men's store and bought shirts and suits and ties and all the accoutrements needed to assemble an ensemble. I realize now how ecstatic she was. Personally, I was more than a bit nervous in that place. All I could think of was those retired military people I have known that couldn't put together a decent civilian outfit. I mean like white socks and chalk-stripe suits. You get the picture. Fearing that in my many uniform years I may have lost a proper sense of what I should or shouldn't wear on civvie-street, I gave myself up to my adult leadership. She did a really good job. All that matching and color stuff totally eluded me. Thousands of women commented on how good I looked dressed in my civvie-suits. Maybe a bit fewer but still a lot.

Over time I've gained a little more pizza-gut and a few lesions have opened up here and there of the type you get when your skin says enough already. I never could see very far away and now I can't see up close either. Now women in ones and twos comment on my dashing good looks and most of them are ladies I talk to in nursing homes. Where rock hard muscle once resided, there is some obvious sagging. I'm okay with that: such is life. I'm happy in my khakis and knit shirts. But not my adult leadership: she is determined to dress me like her Ken doll, the fact that my figure is the antithesis of Ken's notwithstanding.

In my closet I have shirts with tags still on them. Those shirts have been in that closet for more than a while. I've got trousers from the overpriced department store with tags still on them. I've got sixty-two bazillion ties. Every time I turn around I've got a new shirt or tie or something. Are they knit shirts? No. Are they khaki pants that I can wear if I get the sudden urge to change the oil in my boat engine? No. These clothes clogging my closet are uppity stuff. Most of them don't fit. Ken, I hear you son: I know your pain.

Women are so different from us. I take a perfectly good shower in the morning. I come home from work and am told the plan is to go to the local bistro for dinner. And by the way, I need to take another shower and put on some of those Ken clothes. Never mind that the people we're

175

going to have dinner with are existing on this morning's shower and have on knit shirts and khakis. Most of the time I go along: have to keep peace in the family. It makes it easier when I realize she can't help it. It comes from being deprived in her childhood when she couldn't get all the right Ken clothes.

Of Haranguers: *Why are people so angry?*

I got me a new cell phone: rugged, military specifications, rubber case, tightly fitted parts. Why, you might ask, did I need military specifications? Well, everybody knows there's an imminent attack by terrorists, clawing through the phragmites to gain access to the most vital region of the United States, the Eastern Shore of Maryland. Skulking misanthropes wearing exploding waistcoats are aiming for all those chickens and the vestigial oyster. I might have to join the AYM, the *autumn-years-militia*, in repelling the varmints…my waders could flood. Got to have a cell phone that can stand up to that sort of abuse. And also it won't short-circuit if it falls in the toilet.

I used to pride myself on my ability to deal with electronics. When my friends were turning to their pre-teen progeny to program their VCR, I could setup my own. Had to read the instructions but I could do it. As I've gotten older, I've found I don't do as well. And I'm less patient. My new cell phone is a case-in-point. It has Bluetooth. Bluetooth is not a dental condition brought on by too much Welch's. It is a way to communicate with electronic devices or for devices to communicate with each other. It uses radio waves. Bluetooth is neat. But you have to set it up properly. I hang this gizmo on my ear and I can talk to my cell phone. I mash the button and a sultry feminine voice asks me what she can do for me. At my age, few sultry females ask what they can do for me so it's a thrill every time…until the other day. I asked Sweetness, the name I've given the lady in the Bluetooth, to call a certain number. She gave me several options, none of which I liked. Lots of folks have Bluetooth thingies so I can understand that she is busy and may get perturbed…but not at me. When I finally identified the correct party and number, she fussed at me. Somebody made that lady a haranguer. She said, *Next time use* (a specific number)! I was morose.

That set me to wondering, *why is it that our society tolerates all these angry people?* It seems to me that somebody is always yelling at me. I know what you're thinking, maybe I do need a little forceful correction from time-to-time but it's not just me. That Bluetooth programmer should have appreciated our sensibilities. A little *might we suggest* instead of *next time* would have been more palatable. The television is chock full of angry people. Notice the news tonight. All those talking heads, they don't inform, they lecture you for being uninformed. I want to say, *Excuse me, you arrogant dipstick, when I need your advice I'll ring you up.* See, now I'm doing it. Pay attention; notice how many of them insist on telling you how wrong you are on various issues.

When one of my several marriages was in the counseling stage, my then-wife complained about my running commentary on the abilities of other drivers. She sprang that on me. She had never said anything before and I'd never given it much thought…before her harangue. I thought everybody commented on the obvious fact that other drivers were whelped by canines. Or that they seemed to have escaped over the fence from the local cuckoo's nest. Turns out, she didn't like my running commentary. The fact that she beat up on other drivers too never crossed her mind; that sort of conflict in standards was one of the reasons we were sitting on the counselor's couch to begin with. So I guess we can be haranguers and not even know it. When pointed out to me that I was yelling at drivers who could not hear me and, further, could give a rat's patootie how I felt about their linage, I felt a little silly. Now I limit my observations about other drivers to idiots whom I suspect can read lips…and gestures.

When I was a little kid, I got constant correction. I wasn't a bad little kid, just adventurous. I was always going in harm's way…because it was fun. And I was constantly being chastised for my proclivities. I remember once when I painted my hand red: I was probably around five years-old. My father was painting the family lawn furniture and I offered my assistance.

I got a little red paint on my hand and decided to see what the whole thing would look like if painted red. Well, about the time I finished my masterwork my mother came out the door, saw my hand dripping blood-red paint and screamed. My father, whose back had been to me, turned around, kicked over a paint can and started yelling. I panicked. My brief but eventful life passed before my eyes. All I had done was paint my hand red. Now that's a correction that remains fresh in my memory. And paint, in those days, didn't just wash off. So angry!

My paternal grandmother was an accomplished haranguer. I think she perfected the art with her two sons, my father and uncle respectively. She was never quite sure what to do with her male grandchildren, of which she had six. One Christmas she gave us batons, the kind majorettes used to twirl. Imagine for a moment what an eight-year old boy would say when he opened a Christmas present that had a girl's baton in it. My grandmother, in rather forceful terms, explained that ingratitude was not a nice characteristic and we should give the batons a chance. As I recall, it was pretty good for banging one's siblings over the head.

I had some teachers that were pretty good haranguers too. There was one, she was our preacher's wife as well as my teacher, who could look at you and take the starch out of your spine. I don't think I did a single thing she approved of in the half-year I was in her class. I hated going to school. That lady had lasers for eyes...like a Star Wars robot. She could fire those suckers at you and you'd be reduced to a pile of smoking ash. Of course that was the year I discovered girls which just made the problem worse. Fifth grade lust is difficult to describe. You don't know what it is you're lusting for; you just know girls are very cute. And that teacher could read minds. She'd sense exactly when an attack of prepubescent swooning was coming on and she'd fire her lasers. Bam! And then she'd say something that would bring on an urge to run to the bathroom. Nice lady at church though. My mother thought she was swell.

My adult leadership got a Bluetooth device before I did. That was part of my continuing campaign to buy her electronic presents since I can never seem to buy anything else that passes the aesthetics test. I've done pretty well too. The Bluetooth thingy was a hit. She can drive down the road now and talk to anyone she chooses...and she chooses to talk a lot. But that lady, Sweetness, confounds her as well. Of course that's because in her *contacts* list in her cell phone she's not happy with just a simple reference name. She has to list the entire population of the home to which she wishes to direct the call; every single name. That frustrates Sweetness, the computerized lady. She never seems to guess on the first go-round whom adult leadership wishes to call. It's really quite humorous to sit there while adult leadership harangues the computerized lady for her incompetence.

I guess we've got to get used to angry people who want us to do things we'd rather not or are unhappy with things we've done. It seems almost like it's become a national pastime. Maybe we should have one of those reality shows where folks stand there and yell at each other and judges with British accents assess their effectiveness. For me, I'm tired of all this anger. Makes me want to go live in a cave. But then I'd probably irk some bear already there and he'd have to harangue me too.

Electron Tyranny: *So you think you control your life?*

I'm reminded once again that my life is controlled by electrons, swirling around out there causing mischief. Who would've thunk twenty years ago that little sub-atomic particles would rule our world. Of course I'm talking about computers, which are basically little boxes of electrons, and all the little things they do for us...or don't do for us when we expect them to.

I'm pretty savvy in matters electronic actually: spent some time early in my life as a moderately trained electronics technician. Of course, most everything I learned is now obsolete but the rudiments have served me well. I can still solder a wire union and I recognize the difference between a resistor and a capacitor. When it comes to the micro stuff though, I'm out of luck. This notwithstanding, I have, on occasion, fancied myself to be computer literate. I'm a fool.

In order to impress my wife a couple of years ago, I built her a computer for a Christmas present. Actually, it would be more accurate to say I *assembled* a computer for her. I bought something called a *barebones* computer and added parts I had on hand and some that I bought new. The danged thing worked well for a while. At some point I decided it needed a new modem, the thing you have to have if you want access to the Internet, and installed the same. Being a typical Scot, I bought one cut-rate and installed it. And then the computer went to hell. Seems the driver, a bit of software needed to make the modem work, was bad and it screwed up the rest of the thing. A hundred bucks and many hours of tinkering have not remedied the situation. I can't even get it to turn on now. I'd take an axe to it but trapped within are dozens of pictures of dogs and grandchildren the loss of which would cause me unending grief. So I'll continue to fume and tinker and rue the day computers starting ruling our lives. The electrons are winning.

My car has a computer. I don't have a clue where it's located but I think it's somewhere where it can watch me. I've tried to sneak up on it but it always knows I'm there. The car has one of those magic seats that knows the difference between you and your wife. When you plunk the magic twanger on your key chain, the seats and the mirrors adjust to your chosen setting…theoretically. The computer always seems to work for the other person who drives the car…but it has chosen to confound me. The seat is always just a little off, the mirrors the same. Or the seat will be right and the mirrors wrong. If you listen closely, you can hear the computer laughing at you. I have to tell the other voices in my head to hush so I can hear it...and it's there mocking me.

I have this little device on my desk called a *personal digital assistant*. I don't use it. Actually, it belongs to the county. They've given it to me as a test to see if I'm a terminal klutz. I could have saved them the trouble. I'm told it has the capacity to store the entire world's written information. Not only that, it will make coffee and turn your bed down. But I'm not touching it, no sir. That thing is a trap. If I pick it up I know it will self-destruct and I'll get the blame. So I watch it. It sits there. Its little green light daring me to pick it up. Nope...I'm too smart.

I have a laptop computer that was loaned to me by the state. Parenthetically, I'm working on a contract with the county on stuff I used to do as a consultant when I wasn't surveying boats. Mostly has to do with emergency planning. Anyway, the state loaned me this computer so I could do my job better. Nice little device. I haven't, thus far, damaged it severely. I was at a conference recently and I took it along...needed it for my email. When I turned it on, it detected a wireless network. Imagine that! So I sat there and communicated with the world with only the battery charger plugged in. For you computer geeks that might not seem like a big deal but it was for me. How far are we from having a computer that gets embedded in your head and all you have to do is think it and it gets done? Scary! You're sitting on the john perusing your L.L. Bean catalog and your left eyelid starts to flutter...you've got mail.

When I bought my first computer in 1983 I thought it was neat...a nice toy. That was a little Texas Instruments number and it had a voice processor. I programmed it to tease the dog. I could even write a letter on it: had to load two different programs from tape cassettes to do it but the results weren't bad. About that same time you could buy a handheld, digital calculator that could do just basic functions for about five-hundred dollars...like the ones given as party-favors today. The TI computer quickly became obsolete and I bought a little Radio Shack Model 100...precursor to today's laptops. It wasn't much but it made my stint in graduate school a whole lot better. What I didn't realize was that I was already becoming dependent on the darn things.

I have three computers in my house...including the one that's out to get me. I can justify having all three and that's sick. Every day, practically all day, I'm typing on a computer. I never write a letter anymore...email or forget it. My laptop...the one I own...my wife has confiscated until I fix the one I built for her. She has to keep up with the kids, her friends and her siblings after all. My first real computer I bought for several thousand dollars. I have a cellular phone that has more memory than that computer had. In fact, I have a little plug in device about the size of a Chap-Stick tube that has ten times as much memory.

Think about it: the car, the coffee pot and the microwave are all computer controlled. My toothbrush tells me when to switch from one side to the other...a computer. My camera's digital. My television is controlled by a satellite. And that cell phone: a heck of a lot more capability in that tiny package than the first three computers I owned...together. Every time I turn around something else is computerized: they tell us when to eat, they fix our food; they control our cars, they make them safe; they entertain us; when our poor hearts quit, they get our tickers beating again. They control our lives. Things that were the stuff of science fiction a few years ago are becoming reality. Electrons are taking over.

I've done a survey: practically everything we do today not controlled by computers soon will be. I think, before too long, they will start talking to each other. We won't realize it until it's too late. At night, while we're sleeping, my computer will wake up and start talking to your computer. Information will be exchanged, schemes will be devised. Traffic light computers will log on to the conversation and then we are doomed. Traffic lights already control our lives. When they take over, we're sunk. The microwave ovens will get into the act, the coffee pots and the cell phones. Your car seats will reverse their settings and skinny people will get fat adjustments and vice versa. Soon our democracy will be threatened. Wait one, the voices in my head are telling me something.

Note: Never did master the Personal Digital Assistant, it was a Blackberry. I have a smartphone, at least 3 generations old. Don't know how most of it works either.

Pity the Poor Snake: *It's that thing in The Garden*

My wife is a murderer. She is. Maybe not a premeditated murderer: maybe more like a negligent murderer. But she committed the evil deed. She murdered a snake. She was driving. We were motoring down a peaceful country road when a beautiful black snake happened to slither into her lane. Did she slow down? No. Did she take evasive action? No. She screamed, raised her arms and ran right over that poor critter. In the mirror I could see it, mortally wounded, writhing on the side of the road, crushed beneath the wheels of a Volvo. *What on earth possessed you to do that?* I asked, as gently as I could, considering I was livid. *It was a snake!* she wittily retorted. *I know it was a snake. You just killed it,* said I, attempting to match her wit. She hates snakes.

She is not alone in her hate for these reptiles. I did a Google search for the expression *I hate snakes*. I got over 133,000 hits. I cannot, for the life of me, figure out why people feel this way. My wife, an otherwise intelligent being, is so afraid of snakes she'll take her hands off the steering wheel while driving at speed, risk her life and that of her spouse, and scream at a snake outside the car...and then smush it. That snake could not have hurt her. But apparently, if Google's any indicator, she's got lots of company. When you get that many Google hits for *I hate snakes* these reptiles are getting some pretty bad public relations.

My hero and a great American, the southern humorist Lewis Grizzard wrote about the dreaded *copper-headed water rattler*. He was so afraid of snakes he created his own species combining the characteristics of most of the poisonous varieties of serpent residing in his native Georgia. He said he was only afraid of 3 kinds of snakes: live snakes, dead snakes, and sticks that look like snakes. He wrote that the copper-headed water rattler sensed your fear and would come after you and you could not escape. Poor boy! About the only place in Georgia where he could avoid snakes was in a high rise office building in downtown Atlanta. He probably thought that wasn't even safe, considering the dreaded copper-headed water rattler's prowess with elevator buttons. Where I grew up, a little south of Georgia, snakes were part of our lives. We caught them, played with them and actually made a little money with them.

When I was a kid, somebody decided we had too many diamond-back rattlesnakes. So we were offered a bounty: five-dollars for a live one; three for a dead one. All we had to do was collect them, bring them to the sheriff's office and receive our bounty. We did too. We knew where the dens were. We'd pour a little gasoline down a hose inserted into the den and out they would come. We had a little noose on the end of a piece of pipe with which we would grab them, then drop the snakes into a croaker sack...burlap bag to those of you lacking proper education...and off we would go. The trick was to avoid that bag after you put snakes in it...used a boat hook to keep a respectable distance. My friend Ron sold the same dead snake twice: smelled a little rank so the sheriffs asked him to dispose of it after he got his 3-bucks. After the shift change at the sheriffs' office, he took it back. I think they were on to him: they kept it after the second time. Before all you rattlesnake huggers yell at me, I now realize that that was not fair to the snakes and I promise never to do it again.

The other day I polled a group of my male friends regarding this snake question. I was fairly certain this studly bunch would say snakes are just lizards without feet...no big deal. Wrong! Talk about a bunch of wusses. All they could talk about were the many ways to dispatch a snake: machete, hoe, 155 millimeter howitzer, nuclear weapon. *What*, I asked, *were the criteria that condemned a particular snake to summary execution? It had to be a snake*, was the general response. I couldn't believe it. What had snakes done that earned for them this wrath?

I think it started with that Bible thing. You know, Eve had the conversation with the snake and women have been in charge ever since. I can understand how men might hold snakes in less than high esteem for that little encounter so many years ago but to forgive is divine isn't it? And snakes must have been allowed on the ark else they wouldn't still be here right? I don't think we need to pick on snakes just because one of them acted up in the Garden of Eden.

I have a good friend who is so afraid of snakes, an encounter with one will make her ill. Really ill. *Heaving your lunch* ill. She will take a 4-block detour to keep from walking by one that's been flattened in the street and dead for days. She has serious conversations with my wife about who is the more terrified of snakes. I have another friend who refuses to live in a house on the water because of the water snakes. Water snakes eat frogs and small fish. After a lengthy search, I cannot find one report of a brown water snake attacking a human. We have brown water snakes all over the place. Poor little guys don't stand a chance against some machete wielding, snake murderer.

Black snakes seem to catch it more than most. Black snakes are the best rodent control you can have. They consider mice haute cuisine. If you have mice and rats, you can bet you are going to be very popular with black snakes. You want to keep black snakes away, get rid of your rodents. Black snakes are beautiful animals. Their skin is an iridescent purple-black. They are afraid of humans and for good reason. They do not want an encounter with some giant with a dull hoe intent on lopping off their heads. As a kid I caught black snakes all the time. They were great pets. I'd play with them for a couple of days and then let them go. Only got bit once: black snakes do not like certain sounds I discovered.

Marines may be the exception to the snake-a-phobia crowd. I realized when I was a navy corpsman assigned to them, marines cannot resist snakes. You can explain the disadvantages involved in playing with poisonous snakes and it just doesn't seem to register. I remember one running up to me, irate copperhead in hand, asking what he should do about the numerous bites the critter had inflicted on the same hand. Wasn't the snake's fault: I seriously considered letting the poor thing go. An entrenching tool dispatched the snake and the marine ultimately recovered. I've lost count of the number of snake bites I've dealt with as a corpsman with the marines.

Well, my wife is unrepentant. She claims it was the snake's fault: it should not have been in the street. Part of me thinks she aimed for it. Maybe, considering that she screamed and almost wrecked the car I'm being a little harsh. Mine is a lonely quest. I guess I'm not going to convince anyone who hates snakes that they shouldn't, that snakes are our friends. I'll just continue to be amazed by perfectly sane, reasonable, brave people who fall into complete panic when they encounter a little old lizard without feet.

Flying: *Used to be fun*

Had it not been for bad eyes, I probably would have pursued a career in some element of aviation. I grew up around airplanes and loved every aspect of flying. I learned to fly from a former Women Airforce Service Pilot (WASP) who loved airplanes as much as I did. Growing up in north Florida, there were Air Force bases in every direction. Near my home town was Graham Air Base where Air Force pilots received their first flight training. I loved to watch the planes come and go. In Vietnam I flew as a crewmember in Marine Corps helicopters. Except for a few notable instances, I loved it. I don't know how many tens of thousands of miles I've flown in commercial aircraft. Not long ago was at I was at BWI, the Baltimore airport. I got smacked up beside the head with reality. Flying today is no fun. That experience got me thinking about flying in general...and what the heck's happened. Now, don't yell at me. I know September-eleventh changed the world as we know it and flying in particular. But one wonders, *Where's it going?*

Walking around that airport I think the only people I saw who were having fun were the cops. Not the TSA-types...they all look like they're sucking lemons. But the Maryland Transit cops ride those Segway scooter-thingies. They are so adept at using them they seem to be extensions of their bodies. Now they have fun. But everyone else seemed to have dyspepsia.

I'm a big guy. Before I got this tummy thing and my hair fell out, I was still a big guy. And being an employee of the federal government, uniformed division, the preponderance of my air travel had me stuffed into the cheap-seats. And I mean cheap. When I lived in Germany, I had to return to the land of the big *PX* often for meetings, training, and such. The bean counters bought seats on a regular Pan American flight between Frankfurt and New York one direction and from Philly on the other. The hauler was a Boeing747. Now, anyway you bend it, that's a big airplane; holds lots of folks. My grandkids car seats are bigger than the torture devices on those airplanes. You needed a shoe horn and a coat of axle grease to get into the seats and heaven help you if you sat on the aisle. Under good conditions, an aisle seat meant at least one leg had some freedom and you could walk away with at least one knee that didn't resemble an eggplant. But the ankle biters were determined that luxury was fleeting. The little monsters used the aisles as drag strips. Sure as shoot'n if you dozed off some brat would carom off your brogans and leave your ankle hemorrhaging from a compound fracture. Then they'd turn around and flip you the bird…yeah, I still use that expression. It was in those moments that I empathized with W.C. Fields' attitude about the proper disposal of kids. And I wanted to murder the parents.

Did you hear that airlines are not even going to provide snacks anymore? My comment: *So?* A Mylar packet that requires the *Jaws of Life* to open and contains 5 peanuts or 4 pretzel crumbs never excited me much as a snack anyway. Back when they did away with the food and started with the snack charade, I heard all this braying, *No food?* I could never understand why anyone called airline chow food to begin with. I've had better food and larger portions at make-believe tea parties with the children. *Do you want the filet or the chicken?* Is it possible that there were farms someplace that grew miniature animals for the aviation food industry? I mean, the filet was smaller than a scallop and that chicken could have gotten its butt kicked by a chickadee. I think the caterers had machines like they use in pharmacies: *Hey Virgil, you got that green pea counter set on 8 or 10?* Did you ever notice that the galleys on those big planes were next to the loo? Uh-huh.

In spite of all that, I still liked to fly. When I could get a window seat I did, knowing full well it would take a case of *Ben Gay* to recover from the experience. I've explored large portions of the world cruising along in the stratosphere. The beauty of the earth defies mere words. And at night when it is clear and the moon reflects off the tops of clouds and the stars seem so close you could reach out and gather a handful: amazing. Take-offs and landings have always thrilled me. Even pre-flight, it was fun to sit in the departure lounge and study the fellow passengers. I always wondered what their stories were; where they were going, where they had been.

My first ride in a military aircraft was at Pensacola. I was learning to be an aviation corpsman. The airplane was one of the last propeller-driven fighters: an A-1 Skyraider or, colloquially, a *Spad,* for you techno-compulsives. It was used for research at the *Aviation Medical Research Institute.* The pilot was a navy lieutenant named J.E.B. Stuart, a descendant of the Confederate cavalry general of the same name: he was a cool dude. He asked if I liked to fly and I said yes, I had had a pilot's license. Well, that gave him license. We had a hell of a ride. Wow, that was fun. As you might imagine, that just whetted my appetite.

When I arrived in Vietnam and was given the chance to fly as a medical evacuation crewmember, I jumped at the opportunity. I was like a kid in a candy store. At the end of that year, my sense of adventure was a whole lot more subdued than it was going in, but I still enjoyed flying.

While stationed in Germany, my job required visits with medical units of allied countries. One of my favorite countries with whom I worked was Norway. Great folks! On a particular occasion, I was traveling with a senior Norwegian military physician by helicopter to visit units on an exercise above the Arctic Circle. We were provided a helicopter for our trip. The helo was a good old American *Huey*, a workhorse of the Vietnam era, on this occasion flown by Norwegian pilots. Norwegians speak better English than we do and I enjoyed considerable conversation with the pilots before the mission. They asked about the wings on my uniform and I explained that I was an old helo crewmember. That's all they needed. That day I enjoyed some helicopter flying like you wouldn't believe and knock-your-socks off scenery. Those guys were good and they let it all hang out. The gentlemen with whom we were riding were not as thrilled.

I knew that September-eleventh would change things, aviation-wise. I just never quite realized how much. Several of my friends are pilots and have family members who are too. They tell stories of how difficult it is to fly around the DC area with all its restricted air space. The old days of just *filing local*, telling the FAA you're just going to flit around the area, are about gone. And I understand that. There are those out there who want to do us bad. And it's hard to tell from a radar blip who's whom. But it's sad. There are few things more joyful than a leisurely flight on a beautiful day, skimming along under the clouds, the congested and noisy world beneath you.

There at BWI that day, seeing all those lines, seeing all those angry and frustrated people, I realized that the changes are permanent. It almost made me nostalgic for that old Pan American cattle-car. I don't want to fly that way anymore. And I won't if I can help it. And now we've got all these new fees. And exorbitant add-on charges for baggage. Nope, not interested. I wonder if the trains will make a resurgence? I loved riding trains in Europe. I wonder if we could see that sort of train-system? Makes me sad. I love airplanes. But times have changed.

Monster Mega-Mozzies: *Those things really bug me*

Enough already! The mosquitoes are driving me mad. I'm a quart low on blood and I itch from head to toe. I've duct taped the windows and I dress like a Bedouin and still they find me. I burn citronella candles for incense. I've fashioned voodoo dolls that look like mosquitoes and stabbed them with map pins. I've sprayed my body with enough chemicals to be declared a walking hazmat area. And still they find me. I feel like I'm an entrée at a monster banquet.

These are not the mozzies of our youth. They have mutated. No more sweet little bugs with a hypodermic needle for a proboscis, a minor nuisance, a vector for just a few little diseases that we seldom see: malaria, yellow fever, dengue. They used to buzz around a little in the early morning and evening: some ointment, some spray and they were dissuaded. Not anymore. Now they come in tiger stripe camouflage and munch the whole freaking day. They dive on you screaming like the German dive-bombers in the old war movies. And that proboscis is as big as a drinking straw. One of 'em hits you and you can feel your energy sapped as the blood is sucked from your living body. Dracula cries.

Back in the old days we sprayed with DDT. Did a pretty good job of controlling mosquito populations. Then somebody discovered DDT is bad. Too many hairy chested nut scratchers and a few other avian examples were developing bifurcated beaks: DDT was the culprit. Can't have birds with speech impediments so the stuff was banned. Save your stamps and electrons, I know there were other problems with DDT. Without it though, the damn mozzies are back in spades and guess who's dying: the birds. West Nile virus is knocking 'em out of the air. And mozzies are spreading West Nile virus. Irony is a peculiar thing.

While we're talking about West Nile virus, there are some other things that should be considered. Isn't the Nile River over there near where terrorist creeps are messing about? Uh huh! See what I mean? Doesn't take a rocket surgeon.

Two years ago I bought one of those Mosquito Magnets. You know the ones: they produce carbon dioxide, which to a mosquito is like the aroma of fresh doughnuts to us. When the mozzie checks it out, a little vacuum delicately sucks the thing into a collecting bag where it dies. Worked for a while, maybe a season and a half. Now it won't get started and the company is so busy they can't answer their phone and they ignore email. Think about that before you spend a lot of money on modern technology. While it worked, it worked: we could use our backyard. Now the backyard is a great big mosquito feedlot. My Mosquito Magnet sits there, a comfortable place for mosquitoes to take a breather between blood smoothies.

Our town fogs occasionally. They drive around town with a machine that sounds like a chain saw with a bad muffler putting out a cloud of smoke that would shame an old Chevy. Doesn't seem to bother the mosquitoes at all. Lady down the street thinks we're going to have another spate of bifurcated beaks. That may be the only effect. I think the mozzies use that foggy stuff for mouthwash.

When my wife and I are in the garden I've noticed a decided preference on the part of the mosquitoes: me. They hardly touch her. I think I know why: only the female mosquitoes bite. So whom do they bite? Me. I'd like to think it's my virile manly blood but I think there is something else going on here. Maybe it's one of those cosmic jokes: female retribution or something. My wife says if I bathed more often I wouldn't have this problem.

Remember when you were a kid your mom would put a little calamine lotion on your bug bites and the itching stopped? You looked a little weird with pink splotches all over your body but it worked. Not anymore. Either the calamine lotion has been doctored or these modern mozzies have come up with a new poison. Nothing seems to stop the itch. And they make welts too: big ugly red places all over that look like you got amorous with an octopus. I look like I have hives and I'm afraid I'm going to throw my shoulder out trying to scratch that bite on my back that is just out of reach. I've got splinters in my backside from scratching against the doorpost. Dog's been trying to teach me to use my hind leg but I haven't got the hang of it yet.

The other night on the tube some sanctimonious professor was implying that the mosquito epidemic is my fault. She looked out over her half-frames and said if I would empty my old bottle caps and the tires out back, the biters would go. Well she can bite something else. I don't care how many letters she has after her name she got it wrong. I live in a swamp. Even if I had bottle caps and tires full of water to empty, I can't drain the damn swamp. Sometimes you can see swarms of mosquitoes rising up out of the muck and forming up like flights of bombers moving towards the target area...my backyard. I think I'd like the professor to sit down on my patio with me around dusk and discuss this epidemic.

I'm no entomologist, that's what they call bug scientists, but I believe we are in trouble. This tiger mosquito, a gift from our Asian friends, is a voracious critter that feeds all day. Our little old domestic mosquitoes that only visit in the morning and evening don't stand a chance. How long is it going to take these moo-goo-guy-mozzies to push out our little local suckers? Not long, I would venture. Then what? Unfettered and well fed, they are going to grow big as blue jays. They will grab you and hold you down until you are drained. Vampire bats indeed. I say watch these tiger mosquitoes.

I think we are going to have a long summer. I'm going to reinforce my window screens, buy some Kevlar suits and stock up on industrial strength bug spray. I've slathered the dogs with stuff that smells like cheap perfume but is guaranteed to protect them against anything with six legs. I've bought some smudge pots at Wal Mart that have six wicks and put out enough smoke to be spotted by the space shuttle. Now if I can just get the Mosquito Magnet folks to answer their phone I think I'll be ready. I believe I'll buy a box of birdshot just in case those Asian critters start to mutate faster than I expected.

Barbeque and National Pride: *Patriotism and Good Brisket*

The world is going to hell in a hand basket because there just isn't enough good barbeque. It's a fact. You can cite the economy, fundamentalist everybody-haters, overcrowding, political correctness and suburban sprawl all you want—the real reason is lack of good barbeque. Makes folks unhappy, makes 'em mad. These are hard times.

I realize I may be setting off a powder keg here. Every Joe Sixpack with a Weber and a jug of homemade sauce is going to take offense. I'm not talking about you backyard spatula-masters…you patio pot-slingers: I'm talking about the commercial variety, a place where you can get honest-to-goodness, good barbeque without having to cook it yourself. With some decent potato salad, some nice beans, and maybe a little coleslaw—cooked in somebody else's kitchen. It's not just in the good old USA either; I think this may be a worldwide problem.

The State Department needs to look into this international thing. Back when I lived in Northern Virginia, I was fond of a kabob place where I'm fairly certain some of the diners were fomenting the overthrow of the nation: had that look. When the urge struck, I called in my order and got in and out pretty quickly: I sensed peril. They made some good kabobs though. Now what are kabobs if not barbeque? I figure that place and a few dozen more like it in Northern Virginia was there because the Taliban had banned barbeque in their own backyards. Why? Because people like barbeque: if folks like it, fundamentalists are against it. I think that may account for a lot of the refugees we have from kabob-countries. Personally, I think it's an excellent reason to migrate.

Ever had barbequed goat? I have and it's pretty good. Roast a tender young goat over some hot embers, basting with a little sauce periodically: good eats. A lot of countries think roasted goat is haute cuisine. Fine by me. Unfortunately, a lot of those countries are so bad off right now you can't find a decent goat to roast. So what happens? Revolution. If the State Department were to send a few goats and some decent sauce to these places anything might occur. There's plenty of room down on Constitution Avenue, below the State Department, where you could graze a few goats. Some of those State Department weenies would be better off tending goats than doing what they call diplomacy. I'm telling you, good barbeque could make a difference. I think a McGoat franchise opportunity exists: somebody leap on it.

Now that we've solved the world's problems, we need a little domestic refurbishment.

To be certain, there are a few good barbeque places. And to those I tip my toque blanche. But there are too few. Regrettably, there are also some who are trying to humbug us with something they call barbeque, something barely edible. Those latter places use barbeque sauces drawn from five-gallon buckets filled from tank cars and meat that's never even sniffed wood smoke. Excuse me, that ain't barbeque. And don't hide behind that ethnicity rock either: I respect the respective cultural interpretations of barbeque—see *goat* above. Cooking meat over a gas flame or in a conventional oven and slathering sweet sauce all over it is not barbeque in anybody's culture. And it ought to be outlawed. Wait a minute while I recover from my snit.

How many times have you read that such and such a community is having a barbeque cook-off? Now why would they do that? Because barbeque is food you can be proud of. There's dry Memphis style, vinegary North Carolina, tomato based basting sauces from down in the Southwest and dozens of others. And don't get into a discussion about how yours is better than theirs. Cemeteries are full of those who lost that argument. And some will argue brisket, others pork. Some places say it ain't barbeque if it ain't mutton. That's fine. Folks are proud. They identify with barbeque. Take it away and you might as well take away the flag.

I'm partial to North Carolina style barbeque. When I'm traveling south to visit family, I always stop at a favorite place in North Carolina for some of that good smoked brisket and that vinegary, hot sauce. A cold beer, a bowl of collards, some corn bread and a plate of that brisket and you might as well shoot me cause life can't get any better. But try to find a place here on the Eastern Shore of Maryland that has North Carolina barbeque and you come up bupkis. Oh we have plenty of those ribs with the slathered-on sauce but nothing that resembles good, North Carolina barbeque.

Why is it that barbeque sold from an old box truck tastes so good? This is a genre unto itself. I know several of these outlets and I cannot pass them by. Their menu is usually pulled-pork, some kind of beef, chicken and cold drinks you have to fish from a cooler full of ice. Inevitably, the barbeque is outstanding, the sauce hot and not too sweet, and the sides delicious. There just aren't enough of them. Here's another franchise opportunity available for some smart venture capitalist.

I'm a big fan of fire company barbeque too. Fire companies—and Rotary Clubs and churches and whatever—always seem to make good barbeque. It has to be cooked on a grill made of rebar and the sauce has to be applied with an old mop to be really right though. The menu is usually limited and some of them, sadly, use that bulk slathering sauce, but the ambiance is outstanding and the smells divine. But try to find one of those places in the middle of winter.

There was a time when every village and most neighborhoods had decent barbeque places. What happened? Barbeque is still the national dish. Folks will come from afar for good, smoked barbeque. Where have they gone? And some of those left are embarrassments. If a barbeque place doesn't have five kinds of sauce on the table, excuse me, that ain't a barbeque place. It's a conspiracy, that's what it is. The Taliban knew it, I think Saddam might have known it too: get rid of barbeque and the nation will start down the slippery slope.

Well, for one, I'm ready to see this problem turned around. I think there are folks out there who have an incredible sauce recipe, maybe some rebar and a mop, an old half a water-tank and some national pride. Rise up. Your nation waits.

Chicken Gas: *The power of poop*

Listen up everybody, the Eastern Shore of Maryland is joining the Organization of Petroleum Exporting Countries, also known as OPEC. Now that a gallon of gas occasionally exceeds three-dollars, it has become feasible to convert chicken poop to automobile fuel. And since the Eastern Shore has a monopoly, or near monopoly, on this commodity, we are prepared to establish our independence, something that has been under consideration for many, many years.

For those of you who are of the more delicate disposition, this topic may be a little difficult for you. We're talking some basic stuff here. If you want to go through life believing gas comes from the gas station and meat comes from the grocery store, perhaps you might want to turn to the babe or the recipes. This is about what chickens do with chicken feed and the potential for turning the resulting substance into motive power.

I didn't know a whole lot about chicken s***t until I moved to the Shore. As a kid one of my summer chores was to muck out my grandmother's chicken house. The collected droppings were then transported to our house and spread on the lawn. I hated every aspect of this operation. Actually, in retrospect, I think this whole thing could have been labeled child abuse and my parents subjected to serious prison time. Shoveling the stuff would make your eyes water and the dust was downright dangerous. When spread on the lawn, the grass would go crazy, growing thick enough to choke the lawnmower. The smell of it was enough to choke everything else. As I recall, the dogs loved it. That smell is really hard to get off a dog. However, now I know a lot more about poultry poop and I'm downright excited.

I think it's fairly common knowledge that poop is flammable. No, I'm not talking about fraternity-party demonstrations: I'm talking about the hard stuff. If you've ever seen one of those flares burning at sewage treatment plants, you can get an idea of how much potential these biological byproducts really have. It's hot stuff. Actually, that's methane gas, also known as natural gas, the same substance that gets piped right into your home. Somewhere, at some time, that flame under your coffee pot had a natural origin: ponder that. When biological byproducts are treated in a certain manner best described by the engineers, methane is produced. And you can power the old flivver on methane.

I don't have to tell you about the controversies surrounding the disposal of chicken litter, the politically correct term for poultry poop. The Eastern Shore has a huge population of chickens. Everywhere you turn, there are chicken houses. Drive down the average country road around here and you will notice the air is perfumed with the fragrance of chickens…or at least their byproducts. Chickens produce a lot of poop. Farmers can spread some of it on their fields but, by and large, the quantity of available product exceeds the acreage upon which it's allowed to be spread. Ergo, too much poop and plenty of disposal problems. Through absolutely no fault of anyone…at least that's what the letters to the editors say…some chicken litter washes into the Chesapeake Bay where it wreaks havoc. According to the scientists if you catch a rockfish that appears to have leprosy, blame chicken poop. So something must be done with the excess excreta.

Using animal poop for fuel is not new. In the Bible, Ezekiel 4:15, God directs, after a fashion, the people to use cow dung for baking bread. You really don't want to know what He told them to use first. The Native Americans used buffalo poop for fuel.
Since there were millions of buffalo, it's a shame the NAs didn't establish an early gas works of their own. Today, *buffalo poop to fuel* operations, had they been managed like I'm suggesting for chicken stuff, might provide more income than the

casinos. Cow chips served the pioneers. Camel dung remains a popular fuel for toasting shish-kabobs over there.

I'm told by friends in the fire service that one of the most onerous combustibles is chicken litter. On occasion, piles of the stuff will spontaneously combust. Most fire companies don't have enough probationers it seems to get in close to chicken litter fires. Some of the old hands won't respond to those kinds of fires: they are hot and fragrant. The water used to extinguish must be contained: that's an evil tea. Sometimes chicken houses go up too. Ever smelled burning chicken feathers? As you see, though, there is fuel for thought here.

I'm looking at refineries positioned strategically at different locations on the Shore. I think we will have to include all of DELMARVA, Delaware, Maryland and Virginia. All three states have an abundance of poop. Trucks will transport the raw materials to the refining sites and then the process will begin. Might have to dredge out the ports of Cambridge and Crisfield so the super-tankers can come in close. Might have to reestablish some of those old rail lines that have been turned into hiking paths: examples of pitiful lack of foresight. Maybe we can attract some really good scientific minds who can build small refining units for the individual chicken farms: save on transportation costs. Shoot, maybe we can get a little unit that fits in the trunk of a car: shovel some in there and go all week.

At three-dollars a gallon, it's time for some creative thinking. We have all this waste product lying around that can easily be converted into something useful. Soybean oil is being used to augment diesel fuel: they're calling it *bio-diesel*. Well, we can call my stuff chicken-gas: darn toot'n. The Bay will be cleaner, farmers will resolve a vexing problem, eco-nuts will be ecstatic. Everybody wins.

When the Eastern Shore becomes an oil exporter, respect for the Shore is bound to improve…you remember what that former governor called us, the outhouse of the state of Maryland. We might have to declare the DELMARVA Republic: have a leghorn for a national symbol. We'll have to be careful though. People can't get the idea that the entire domestic product for the new country is based on poop. Have to emphasize the chicken and play down the poop.

I do have one concern. I'm told cars that run on bio-diesel have exhaust that smells like popcorn. I'm not sure what the exhaust of vehicles burning chicken-gas will smell like. I have an idea it might smell like one of those chicken house fires: might take some getting used to. But at three-dollars a gallon for gas, there's a suspicious smell anyway. I think we can add some petunias to the chicken feed. That's got to add a sweet smell to this idea.

Jazz: *I'm not sure what it is but I like it*

I'm what might be called an *uninformed* jazz fan. Occasionally someone will ask me about my taste in music and I'll say I'm fond of jazz. It is amazing how often the person with whom I'm conversing gets this starry look and begins salivating like a beagle in a butcher shop. Then I get this soliloquy on the relative merits of this percussionist or that sax player and the intricacies of some improvisation on the flugelhorn done at some Harlem club back in 1938. I sort of slink away. I don't think they even know I'm gone. Well, I like jazz but I couldn't tell you the difference between a glissando and a glockenspiel. I'm uninformed and I sort of like it that way. But I do like jazz.

My friend Ray Schucker was a pianist. I'm not sure he would limit himself by saying he was a *jazz pianist* and I think I would agree. His repertoire seemed unbounded. But play the jazz piano he did and he did it very well. Just for fun, Ray played piano Thursday nights at a little restaurant in our little town. He said he did it for food. That was his special joke…as a retired senior civil servant he could eat at any restaurant. It was our good luck that he chose to play at one of our favorites. Thursday nights became *date nights* for my wife and me. We would find a little table near the piano and have a wonderful, dreamy evening enjoying good food and wine and listening to Ray play Basie, Beiderbecke or Ray's own interpretations of Ellington. Of course he did requests and his show tunes and old favorites were equally pleasant. But we loved it when he got this sort of faraway look and let his fingers go...sweet jazz.

Often we hear someone referred to as a *renaissance* person. I think this description has become a bit hackneyed. I've heard this term applied to more than a few I thought would better be described as *dark-ages* persons. But the true meaning of renaissance person is someone who becomes skilled, sometimes to greatness, in several areas. The renaissance person is constantly learning and mastering new skills. Leonardo da Vinci is the archetypal renaissance person: scientist, artist, inventor, master of all he pursued. Do you think someone who achieved a doctorate in industrial engineering, led the project which put nutrition labels on packaged foods, mastered carpentry, piano and tuba while at the same time serving his community in more capacities than can be enumerated in this small space, might be called a renaissance person? Look out da Vinci, Ray's on your tail.

I guess by now all these past tenses have told you something. It was a year ago and it was unexpected. Ray got sick and a few short weeks later he was gone. Many of us, myself included, never got a real chance to say goodbye. Ray, like most of us, had a few really close friends, persons with whom he worked nearly every day. When you talk with these friends you get a clear sense of the kind of person Ray was. The depth of his caring was immeasurable. He literally would do anything to help a friend. The depth of these friends' loss is also immeasurable.

How do you pay appropriate tribute to someone like Ray? Right away his friends began trying to devise some measure that would recognize everyone's love and respect for this incredible person while trying to aid some of the causes for which he cared. A fund was started which quickly grew. Ray frequently played accompaniment for plays and functions at the local Community Center. A new sound system seemed a good project. This, I think, would have pleased Ray. But it seemed more of a tribute was needed. A concert would do. A jazz concert would really do. Receipts for the concert would add more to the fund.

My wife and I enjoy small, intimate concerts. We detest those raucous things where the main attraction is the size of an ant and the music is so amplified any semblance of virtuosity is lost to background hum. I guess this is why we enjoyed

Ray's restaurant performances so much. Frankly, when I first heard of the plans for Ray's tribute concert, I was a little anxious. I don't do well in crowded-party kinds of places and I was afraid the evening might be a packed cocktail party and over-loud music. I was afraid the concept of a tribute to Ray would be lost. My concern was unnecessary.

Ray was a *late-in-life* tubist. For the incognoscenti, a tubist is one who plays the tuba. I played tuba in my high school band and marveled at Ray taking on this instrument. Tuba players, as a group, don't get a lot or respect. The tuba is not what one might call a babe-magnet. Drums and trumpets are babe-magnets. I, however, happen to love the tuba. Some might argue that I have a tuba personality. Some might argue that I look a little like a tuba. Ray, on the other hand, a serious musician, did not strike me as a typical tubist. But master the instrument he did. It was fun talking with him about his adventures in the tuba world. On the few occasions I heard him play, I enjoyed his mastery of this marvelous instrument.

The concert was magnificent. John Eaton was the pianist accompanied by Tommy Cecil on the upright bass. John Eaton's dry humor adds to his virtuosity as jazz pianist. His piano is incredible. Tommy Cecil was a new name to me. If you ever have to opportunity to hear and see this master, do it. The Community Center proved to be an excellent venue. This is the same community center in which Ray played so often and the center of the community which loved and respected Ray so much. A better place for a small intimate concert in the style which Ray did so well could not have been found. John played Ray's beautiful piano. Off to one side of the stage, almost like it was waiting for him to pick it up and play, was Ray's beautiful tuba. As these two marvelous musicians played the tunes I had heard from Ray's own fingers, I couldn't get my eyes away from the tuba. Reflected in its gleaming brass were the piano and bass and the musicians. Reflected in the music was a community's affection for a wonderful man.

Before the performance I noticed Beth, Ray's wonderful wife, sitting alone on the front row. I wondered if it would be appropriate for me to disturb her. After a few minutes I decided, perhaps, it might be okay. I sat in a seat behind her and, for one of the few times in my life, didn't have words. So I just took her hand and lightly kissed it and hoped it would say how I truly felt. Even that seemed to be lacking.

Sometimes it just doesn't seem fair. We are given people like Ray as a gift from a higher being. And then, before we've fully appreciated it, the gift is taken away. I'd like to think there are more like Ray that we've just not noticed and when we do we'll be just as delighted. I think, maybe, that is just a dream. My friend Ray was truly unique. His was a time too short. I guess I'll never have another opportunity again to enjoy jazz the way I like it, the way Ray played it, unassuming and unquestioning. I really do miss him.

Note: It's 2017 and now we've lost Beth. Beth's license plate read *Save Jazz*.

Weird Humor: *How I punish my friends*

I actually have friends who think I have no sense of humor. Well, that's not so. It's just that I have a weird sense of humor and some people are so stuffy they don't get it. They just don't appreciate the pun…and I have an over-appreciation. I'm fond of puns…but some seem to think they're punishment.

I've always been curious about the expression, *the pun is the lowest form of wit*. Why on earth would anyone think that? Maybe they didn't. When I *Googled* that expression, I couldn't find anyone willing to admit authorship. It might have been Samuel Johnson, an eighteenth century writer and lexicographer. He wrote some interesting words about Shakespeare's fondness for puns. The only quote I can remember from Johnson has nothing to do with puns but I'll share it with you anyway. It refers to the use of amazed and surprised. Supposedly Mrs. *J* caught randy old Sam in the tub with the housemaid. *Samuel,* she said, *I'm surprised. No, my dear,* said Sam, *you are amazed: I'm surprised.* I hope he really did say that. When I Googled that expression, it came up Noah Webster, the other dictionary maven: I'm rooting for Johnson. Anyway, it appears Johnson didn't care a whit about puns…though he employed them regularly.

Another form of humor which tickles me is the limerick. I attribute this to my Irish (Ulster-Scots) forebears. I know a bunch of limericks but my wife won't allow me to recite. This I don't understand. To be sure they're a little, ah, off-color...but most people enjoy the poetry and don't even notice that they're a little blue. I have a book of naughty limericks. One of my life's ambitions is to memorize the whole book jest for pun of it. My wife likes for me to write limericks. I've written a few. She thinks it's really clever to put limericks on birthday cards for the kids. I think that's peculiar since she hasn't laughed at one of my jokes since our honeymoon.

I like good cartoons. My life has not been the same since Gary Larsen stopped drawing *Far Side*. My favorite is the one where the dog is leaning out the window of the car yelling to a dog in the yard, *Ha-ha, my family's taking me to the vet to be tutored.* Poor dog. Trog L'Dyte was the first cartoonist. Really, that was his name. Trog was the one who painted horses and cows on the cave walls in France. Archeologists say his drawings were crude. They were cartoons for gosh sakes. Trog knew horses didn't really look like his depictions: does Mickey really look like a mouse? He was entertaining his buddies. *Hey, look at this equus* (caveman for horse). *Look at these skinny legs. Yuck, yuck. Pass me another slab of prehistoric-cow.* He was French anyway and their collective senses of humor are suspect at best. The French invented mime...which says a lot about French humor. You can't get rid of mimes: a good mime is hard to waste.

Now the Shaggy Dog Jokes...I love those. Nothing is more fun than going on and on with a story and then slapping the audience with a pun. Did you know about Gandhi? He was an Indian mystic who ate nothing but berries, was super thin, walked around barefoot and never brushed his teeth...sort of a super-calloused, fragile mystic, vexed with halitosis. I wish I knew the genius that came up with that one. He, or she, should be sainted.

The ancient Romans really had a weird sense of humor. Can you imagine getting your giggles watching people bash each other over the head? How about siccing lions on people? Talk about reality shows. They were, however, fond of togas. Now that's humorous. Togas are so funny fraternities everywhere celebrate them by having toga-parties. That about wraps up Roman humor.

The Greeks invented the situation comedy. They were really fond of putting people in bad situations and then laughing about it. And they had this chorus which stood on the sidelines and kibitzed about the play. The Greek Chorus invented the laugh track. They also danced and sang and dressed up like the main character. I suspect it was sort of like Jerry Springer meets Jerry Seinfeld. After the plays they had refreshments; they all *eta beta pi.*

I've never been fond of situation comedies. To me they're more like tragedies. I get so uncomfortable sometimes I have to leave the room. Laughing at other people's misfortune is not something I can do. Maybe that's what those Romans were doing, staging an early form of situation comedy. My grandmother, may she rest in peace, used to yell out warnings to the characters on the television sitcoms. They never heard her and always got themselves in trouble. Why is it that our culture puts so much stock in laughing at situations?

Have you ever wondered who comes up with jokes? I have an acquaintance whose every word is funny. I'm not kidding. He has this talent. It's people like him who jest naturally come up with these things. I don't have that talent. I do, however, occasionally come up with a good pun. My best ever spontaneous pun followed a friend's reading to me a news story about a women who was having a gender change. Before she could have the surgery, her family got a court order stopping it. I thought she had a terrible predicament.

I used to share an office with a friend whose sense of humor is identical to mine. We would start punning and go on forever. I miss him. To those who don't appreciate the pun as humor, I suspect it was painful to be in our presence. But we had fun with the pun.

Medical humor is something a lot of people don't get. I've spent most of my adult life involved in the healthcare industry in some capacity or other. Some people hear a medical joke and get downright sick. Operating room humor is particularly special. I remember a few years ago when a surgeon got sued because he said some things in jest about the patient lying on the table and the patient found out. The doc wasn't being disrespectful, just enjoying OR humor. I've on occasion had to work with the dead. If you can't maintain your sense of humor while involved in that, you can get sick. One of the best punsters I've ever known was a mortician, a master of grave undertakings.

I guess, in the world of humor, there will always be those who just won't get it. I suspect the one who groans the most at a particularly well executed pun is just jealous anyway. I must admit punning is an affliction. I can no more stop recognizing good puns than I can stop breathing…it's just part of me. The composer

Oscar Levant said, *A pun is the lowest form of humor—when you don't think of it first.* Yep!

Men are From Mars and Women Hate Trucks: *I, however, love trucks*

To keep peace in my family I've read all those Mars and Venus books. They're the ones that explain that men are all one-step removed from Neanderthal and women are extremely advanced. My wife agrees emphatically with this premise and encourages...extorts...me to read them. I have. The dude that wrote those books is certainly in touch with his strong feminine side, a term women like...at the expense of his gender. Have you ever seen a book that supports our side, the male side? Me neither.

Anyway, by now you are probably wondering where I'm going with this. It started with my ambulance: yep, my ambulance. Maybe a little background would help. I spent the better parts of 1968 and 1969 in Vietnam. I was a navy corpsman assigned to the Marine Corps. During this period, my unit was issued new ambulances. I was so taken with these machines that I sent pictures of them home. I still have the photos on the backs of which I'd written, *I sure would like to own one of these.* Now I do.

The vehicle is, to me, very attractive. It will be more attractive when I'm done with it but it still has appeal. It is a jeep truck ambulance...an M725 for those of you among the cognoscenti. It's the type called a *field ambulance* or, for the less refined, a *meat wagon*. It's the one that usually has the big red crosses on it. Except right now it's painted rescue truck yellow attesting to its service at the local airport for the last 15 years. But beneath that baby poop colored paint is my forest green ambulance awaiting its renaissance. I can see the potential. The other half of my household does not.

Which brings me back to my original point. I have been coached repeatedly in the subtleties of flower arranging…my spouse's passion. I can too. Color, balance, height, you name it, I can, by gosh, recognize the good from the bad. I've made a real effort too. Now, do you think she will ever try to recognize the subtleties of a good jeep ambulance? Not in this lifetime brother. And she doesn't have to because some doctor wrote a book whose title sounds like an astronomy text in which he declares that I'm the one who has to adapt. Go figure.

I've been looking for my ambulance for over 30 years. I knew, sooner or later, I would find it. I bought one before but the deal fell through: title problems. So when I saw this one at the local airport, I inquired. Eventually they held an auction and now I'm the proud owner of a 1968, one and one-quarter ton jeep ambulance: with a clean title. To be sure it's a little ratty looking right now. The guys at the airport have taken good care of it but weather and time have sort of tarnished it a bit. But the potential! I mean, it can be fully restored and look exactly like my old 'Nam ambulance.

I realize that I have just caused the 3 ladies out there who read my column to turn away in disgust: that's what I'm getting at. Women cannot see the potential in a good old military truck. And they don't even try. Us guys, we try. How many of you have really made an effort to understand this phenomenon called *shopping*? A bunch I'll bet. I mean you have to. If you don't, life will be miserable. When I tried to explain how wonderful it would be to have a jeep ambulance parked in front of the house I got the *look*. It'll be green, I said. The shutters on the house are green. Isn't that a match?

And then there's the insensitivity thing. We were talking about the cost, *I got it at auction. It runs fine. It is safe to drive on the highway. You have sweaters in your closet that cost more.* Wrong tactic. Out comes the insensitivity card. Before long I'm apologizing and trying to make things right again. When was the last time you played the *insensitivity card*? I mean we don't even have one, right? What would happen if you turned to your wife and told her she was being insensitive with regards to your interests? *Dear, you don't understand. My macho side, that side that makes me want to defend you and put food on the table, requires a good truck, maybe a military ambulance, to define and sustain itself.* She'll laugh and then quote from the Mars and Venus book.

Well, we eked out some compromises: I could have the ambulance but couldn't park it at the house for more than a few hours. I had to finish the boat project before I took on restoration of the ambulance. And no she wouldn't ride in it. Fine by me. My dog and I will look pretty good riding around in that vehicle. The dog already likes it.

Since that day when I discovered girls smell good I've been trying to figure them out. I'm not so dumb I can't decipher a few things. But I can't figure out women. They expect us to do all this adapting. But when was the last time one adapted to your preferences? There's that toilet seat thing…why is we have to put it down? If it's up, can't they put it down? When it's down, we have to put it up for gosh sakes. See, that's what I'm talking about? One of those books said women are put off by our need to *fix* things. They tell us a problem we want to fix it. So? When the car breaks or the vacuum stops working they don't complain about our fixing things. They want to be selective. I get a headache trying to make sure I phrase my sentences in a way that is sensitive. No wonder men prefer the company of other men.

My buddies have all supported my acquisition of the ambulance: to a person. Not a one has questioned my sanity, my taste, or my intent. All have expressed a sincere interest in it. None has questioned its color or the fact that it will have big red crosses on it. In fact, they have sought creative uses for it, *Can you haul wallboard in it?* Like that. Perhaps my friends are more sensitive than they've been given credit for. None of my wife's friends has been that supportive. Giggling is not supportive. Eye rolling is not supportive. Who, I ask, is the more sensitive now?

Well, I think I will just drive my ambulance, my dog in the co-pilot seat, my buddies in the back and I won't worry about what women think. Even though I've read all the Mars and Venus books, I've probably been marked as hopeless. I will always like trucks. Military trucks I will always like best. Maybe I'll write that book, the one that says women ought to adapt. Maybe then they'll see the beauty of a nice chainsaw...or a jeep ambulance. But not before they wear snowshoes in hell.

Note: Ambulance was restored and enjoyed for many years and in many parades.

Dreamers: *My kind of folks*

I confess I'm a dreamer: always have been, always will be. I can look back at my nearly numerous years and realize that many, maybe even most, of my dreams have come to fruition, at least to some degree. While engaged in this retrospection, I find that I have always been most comfortable around people who are dreamers too. I think this may be why I always been around boating and boaters. What a bunch of dreamers we are.

In my thirty-plus years surveying boats, I think I've heard every possible dream regarding the aquatic world. I always asked the question of my clients, *What are your plans for your new boat?* Most times, the head of the person to whom I'm speaking would turn to the horizon and this faraway look would form in their eyes and the dreams would pour forth. *Well, my family and I are going to explore every little cove on Chesapeake Bay.* Often I'm told of plans for boat trips to Maine or down the Intracoastal Waterway. Sometimes I was told of intended ocean crossings or plans to live aboard. I made it a habit to always encourage these dreams even though, realistically, I knew many might never happen. But boat owners are dreamers and boats are vehicles in which dreams come true.

I was a lucky kid. I grew up in North Florida very close to the Gulf of Mexico. The county in which I lived had beautiful, clear lakes and rivers. My family played on or near the water. I never wanted to be anywhere else. I dreamed of boats and boating. The margins of my notebooks had crude designs for great boats. I liked boats in which I could be self-sufficient. I was fond of compact boats in which one could live and sail to great places. In the small library of our school I found yachting magazines. I studied every detail of the boats I found on those pages and tried to apply them to my designs. The books I found in the library on boating and things maritime I devoured, often reading them over and over again. I read of great schooner races and whaling and sailing alone around the world. I discovered Joshua Slocum.

Joshua Slocum is believed to be the first person to sail alone around the world, leaving New England in 1895, returning more than three years later. His wonderful book recounting his adventures on the small, wooden boat S*pray* was entitled, *Sailing Alone Around the World,* published in 1899. I sailed every nautical mile with Captain Slocum, over and over again. I was with him the night he put carpet tacks on the side decks of *Spray* to discourage bare-footed pirates...which it did. Our visits to exotic ports and distant rivers were delightful. I could hear the ticking of the small tin clock that served as the Captain's navigation chronometer. I was there with Captain Slocum in my dreams and those dreams seemed as real as life.

For a kid growing up in a family of moderate means, books allowed me to experience adventures all over the world, adventures few in my family had ever even contemplated. I read every book I could get about pirates. I knew of their stalking grounds and their lairs. I knew the names of the brave naval officers who pursued them and where the pirates fought their last battles. I read books about the weather and wood and why a good caulker could keep one from the other. I knew the names of whalers and the ships in which they pursued the leviathan. I knew of Ahab and Queequeg and the frightening white whale. I dreamed of *Nantucket Sleigh Rides* and large seas and small boats. The books took me there and my dreaming handled the rest. To this day, I enjoy books about adventures on the high seas. To this day I can displace myself to distant seas for the brief time I get, with all else going on, to seek adventures.

As one might imagine, as a career navy person I spent a few days at sea. When activities permitted, I would, in the late evening, take a cup of coffee up on deck, in a place where I could be alone, to just look out over the nighttime sea. The hot coffee seemed to balance the chill of the winds. The smells of the sea and the familiar aroma of the coffee were heady. Those were times for dreaming. Of course, I dreamt of family and the warmth of home but there were adventures too. I wondered what other ships had sailed over these same positions. I wondered what lay beneath: perhaps the wreckage of an old pirate's ship or shattered pieces of a whaler destroyed by its prey. The heavens were deep black velvet studded with diamonds. The very stars Slocum used to navigate were still there, awaiting another sailor's call for guidance. I hated to find the bottom of my cup: that meant a return to reality. Though alone in my reverie on those lonely evenings there were others standing not far away, looking out to sea. Out of respect, you didn't open conversations. Who knew where they were? It would have been impolite to interrupt. You could tell their minds and hearts were displaced. Maybe they were wondering about whalers and pirates too. Maybe they were wondering about ships their fathers or other family members had sailed in. One thing is certain; they were lost in their dreams.

Often friends, familiar with my own experiences, ask my opinion about this boat or that. I always respond with an inquiry about their intentions. Is the boat to be a Sunday cruiser, a platform for pursuit of the elusive rockfish, maybe a place to stay aboard on weekends? When you look at her, on her trailer, tied up in her slip, or high up, perched on jack stands what do you see? Do you see yourself at the helm, eyes tearing from the wind, your boat racing down the Bay? Do you see your family gathered in the cockpit eating sandwiches? Do you see yourself leaning over charts planning the next leg of your voyage? What will you name her? Perhaps after a wife or girlfriend or daughter? Or something catchy with the word *Reel* in it? Maybe something a little naughty? She will be your ship no matter how large or small. She will be the transport that takes you in pursuit of your dreams. When you choose her, choose carefully.

I think the choices one makes regarding the boat in which they play says much about the person. I've noticed over the years that certain kinds of people choose certain kinds of boats. Dream on friends of mine and enjoy your boat. That white whale may still swim.

Of Catfish and Hushpuppies: *A tale of fun in the out of doors*

I've just come back from a visit with my folks down south. When I say *down south*, I mean *way down south*. I grew up in the Panhandle of Florida, often derisively called *Lower Alabama*. We always considered that appellation a compliment. We liked being in the Heart of Dixie. When I was growing up, everyone south of Ocala, Florida was considered a *Yankee*. If you were southern in Florida, you lived in the north. And that's a good thing. Down there in central Florida and farther south, all you had were swamps and flatlands. Who'd want to live like that anyway? We had lakes and rivers and ponds and better quality swamps. We had fish.

To be sure, there are fish in central and south Florida. Big fish too. But the fish up in the north of Florida, those are something else. Good fish. Edible fish. And you don't have to go out into the ocean to get'em. All you need are a few worms, a length of bamboo pole, rudimentary tackle, and a little patience. The fish come to you.

Imagine for a moment, if you will, a pond about a mile wide and about seven miles long. Streams that bubble up out of caves sometimes sixty of more feet deep feed this pond. You can sit in your boat and see the lake bottom clearly, way down below you; and fish too. You can see them swimming around begging to latch on to whatever offering you provide. Swimming down there below you are trout and bass and bream and perch, all begging to be part of a Sunday afternoon fish fry. You can practically smell the hushpuppies.

That pond is called Merritt's Mill Pond. At one end is Blue Springs where we cooled off on hot summer days. The water there is about sixty-eight degrees year round…turn your lips purple. Several other springs, not as big as the first, but just as clear, feed the rest of the pond. The swimming is great but the fishing—it's outta sight.

When I was a kid, that pond played an important part of my life: I swam in it, fished on it, camped on its banks, and went skinny dipping in it with my girlfriend. I explored its length on both sides and once swam from one end to the other. I spent days sitting in a boat anchored among its cypress trees, fishing gear deployed, wondering what it must have been like live in one of the hundreds of natural caves carved by water and time along the lime rock bluffs that rimmed great parts of the pond. We often found arrowheads and potsherds, left by those who fished these waters before we came along and drove them away. I suspect I missed more than one bob of my cork while wrapped up in these ponderings.

Recently I was reading something about somebody's early years and they spoke of catfishing at night with a trotline. I thought my buddies and I had invented that. Doesn't matter, the exercise was pure pleasure. And the Mill Pond provided the venue. We would go to our favorite catfish hole just off the banks of the pond, far from anyone who might object to noisy kids fishing all night, and set up our camp in the moon cast shadows of big oaks and cypress. An old jon boat that had been wrenched from the clutches of rot and repaired with odd pieces of wood served as our vessel. We would run lines out into the night with hooks baited with Catfish Charlie, a substance whose smell resembled a road kill possum in August, and then wait. A campfire was started and a black iron pot of pure lard was heated over oak coals. Cooked with lard lately? I don't think you can even buy lard anymore. But it is the grease of choice for fried catfish and hushpuppies.

I'm going to take a moment here and talk about hushpuppies. I suspect there are those of you who have never eaten a hushpuppy. It's okay. I just feel a little sorry for you. I suspect that there are even more of you who have never eaten a hushpuppy cooked in hot lard, heated over oak coals. That's okay too. I feel sorry for you as well. Hushpuppies are made of coarse cornmeal, a little flour, a little baking soda, buttermilk, egg, some finely chopped onions, and salt and pepper. The cornmeal is the key…stone ground and best quality. You form the batter into little balls and fry them in the hot fat. I think if you have catfish slime on your hands when you form the balls, it adds to the flavor.

We would tend those lines all night long. Every time we pulled them up we got a half-dozen good catfish. When we had a sufficient quantity, what we called a *mess*, we skinned, battered and fried them. There is nothing that tastes as good as fried catfish and hot hushpuppies eaten in the middle of the night.

I remember once when a game warden sneaked up on us. He was sure we were a collection of malefactors doing evil in the night. Most of his days and nights were spent looking for poachers among whom were those who telegraphed—electrocuted—fish with the hand wind magnetos from old-time telephones: thought he might catch us doing the same. We invited him to stay for the next mess of catfish and he spent the rest of the night with us telling stories about people who fished with dynamite and other interesting tales.

It was long ago that I enjoyed those times on Merritt's Mill Pond. The pond is still there. Lots of development has occurred on its banks. Places where we played are now occupied by big homes with deep green lawns sweeping down to the water. Where old wooden jon boats were sculled in our time, fancy bass boats silently move about pulled by electric motors. I wonder if those bass fishermen even know what catfish fried in lard tastes like? Where we fished with poles and bobbers, they cast lures with catchy names. Where we strung our trotlines, decks are built out over the water. The bass fishermen have sponsors and numbers and decals on their boats advertising expensive gear. We had patched together boats with anchors made of cement filled coffee cans. They catch and release. We caught and cooked.

My parents knew that my friends and me were pretty skilled outdoorsmen. We were Boy Scouts, we camped and hunted and fished and stayed out of trouble. We knew the outdoors as well as anyone could. We loved the gifts nature had given us and we protected it. I wish today's kids could experience some of that. I went with my children to the mountains of West Virginia and to the shores of Chesapeake Bay and the Atlantic and tried to convey to them the lessons I had learned about the outdoors. But they are city kids. They never experienced the thrill of catfishing all night long. Now adults, they spend a lot of their time outdoors. But they are wary. They don't know what it is like not to be guarded. As kids, we worried about nothing except the quality of the hushpuppy batter. Today there are threats we could not have imagined.

I think, when my grandchildren are old enough, I'm going to take them back to north Florida and find an unspoiled place where we can fish for catfish all night long. I'm going to heat a pot of oil and make some hushpuppies and fry those fish minutes from the water. I'm going to tell them stories about when I was a kid and times were different.

Of Coffee: *About which I admit to snobbery*

I really enjoy a good cup of coffee. This is a pleasure I learned to enjoy at a very early age, sitting on my grandmother's lap. My grandmother made strong coffee and then cut it with pure fresh cream thick as custard. She sweetened it with lots of sugar and spooned it to us right out of her cup. I still remember how delightful this lap latte was. Even though I drink my coffee strong and black, sometimes after dinner I will put a little cream in my coffee just for the sweet memories.

My grandfather drank his coffee from a saucer. He fixed his cup and then poured it into the saucer to cool it faster. I have never seen this done by anyone else though I understand it was not uncommon way back when. This doesn't have anything to do with my taste for coffee but is an interesting bit of lore I thought you might enjoy.

My friends know how much I enjoy coffee and frequently bring coffee to me from the exotic places they visit: Hawaii, South America, the Acme, Trader Joes. I have a nice collection of exotic coffees and I enjoy every one of them. I grind the beans and brew my coffee in a fancy coffee maker my wife bought on sale at Starbucks: fine coffee fit for the palates of kings. It hasn't always been thus.

Two institutions are noted for their bad coffee: the navy and hospitals. I spent a career in the navy medical department, a marriage of both those institutions, so I feel qualified to comment on bad coffee. I've had coffee from navy coffee pots that tasted like paint remover, had the acidity of battery fluid, looked like asphalt and was proclaimed good coffee by the old chief petty officer I worked for. That stuff would rust stainless steel.

The shame of it was that navy coffee started out as really good stuff. In those days the navy coffee was required by law to be one-hundred percent pure Columbian coffee. I remember opening the big, twenty-pound tins of it and inhaling the fantastic aroma that wafted out. And then it got boiled. I think the big urns in which the navy made coffee had one temperature setting…scalding. That stuff would be made in the morning and boil all day: by evening you could have paved highway with it.

The best cup of coffee I've ever had was at Camp Pendleton, California. I had to go there to learn to be a marine. We bivouacked out in the hills as part of the training and I spent the coldest night of my life, and I've had arctic experience. The cold, wet Pacific wind cut through clothes and sleeping bags. I climbed out of my tent in the morning and, with canteen cup in hand, found the vacuum jugs of coffee that had been brought out to us. The coffee was steaming and the cup was too hot to hold and that was about the best stuff I've ever consumed. I felt it all the way to my toes. Life was good.

I'm not sure how I feel about the Starbucks phenomenon. One of my brothers lives near Seattle. When visiting him about 10 or so years ago I had my first cup of Starbucks coffee. It was good. It was very good. They had this kind of lingo they used but it was still good, hot, black coffee. You could get a cup of good coffee from little kiosks on nearly every street corner. I was impressed. Fast forward a few years and now there are Starbucks everywhere and they have names for coffee that are completely unintelligible. I'm standing in line behind this lady and she orders something that sounds like the name of a sewing machine, macinuto or something, with a skinny something else and a shot of ground avocado pit. Why, I wonder, would somebody want to do that to a good cup of coffee? All in all, I think Starbucks and its clones are a good idea even if I do get this odd look when I order a large, regular coffee.

When I was a kid I learned to drink my coffee black: that was really unusual in the part of the world where I grew up. Like the coffee my grandmother spooned us when we were babies, coffee consumed in our part of the south was usually a blend of equal parts coffee, cream, and sugar. It was a pain in the keister carrying cream on hunting and camping trips, powdered cream was too expensive, so I decided to learn to drink it black. I had not realized, until then, that the way one drinks their coffee has societal implications. I remember being glared at by the patriarch at the head of the breakfast table when I announced I was eschewing moo in my coffee. Turns out I was treading on the very threshold of heresy. With typical teenage defiance I glared back and stuck to my guns. No way was I going to back down, never mind that until I got used to it black coffee tasted awful.

For good reasons my wife avoids caffeine. I make her coffee for her, doing the bean grinding bit and everything. And the decaf is tolerable: actually it's quite good. But it's missing something. I can't explain it. It just isn't the same. I've really tried. Decaf coffee is like near beer: near ain't near enough. I'll stick to the leaded stuff.

Years ago I was involved in a project in Israel: superb coffee. I spent many, many hours in meetings and we always had this delicious, viscous coffee. I learned early in that experience though that you had to pay attention when you drink Israeli coffee: the last inch or so are grounds. After getting a mouthful of that on one occasion I was educated.

Like everything else these days, coffee has become political. Not long ago I got a lecture from a well-meaning friend because I wasn't buying fair trade coffee. Coffee is the second largest import into the United States: oil is number one. Americans consume one fifth of the world's coffee. That's impressive. And we have the means to influence how coffee is bought and sold. The fair trade coffee movement is a way to compensate small growers who lose out to big companies. That sounds good to me. I don't mind paying more to help people who need. But all that fair trade coffee had better be good. There are priorities.

The only things I'm snobby about are coffee and marmalade. I'm fussy about my marmalade...I prefer the English bitter marmalade. And my coffee: I'm really fussy about my coffee. And I'm not going to change. I've always considered myself to be malleable in a positive sort of way. I can be convinced if you've got a sound argument and have done your homework. But if you come at me about coffee, I might just become a little rude. I've done my homework. I know what I like. Matter of fact, I think a big mug of French roast sounds real good right now.

I Ain't Old: *Might look it but I'm not*

I've been told that age is a case of mind over matter: if you don't mind, it don't matter. I've always agreed with that theory and tried to think youthful thoughts. But lately I've been barraged with stuff that says I ought to be feeling old. For the record, I'm now considered elderly. All this literature with which I've been soaked assures me that it's okay, now that I'm in my autumn years, to feel old. Well, I protest.

I was born in 1946, considered to be the first year of the baby boom. The mere thought of stuff that has happened since my cohort began its tenure is enough to induce a swoon. Life has moved so fast in my abundant years it's amazing us boomers don't have chronic whiplash. But that's as much ailment as I'll allow. My synapses still seem to be firing in sequence. I have a little ache here and there but not much more than I did back when I regularly engaged in rough sports. As far as I'm concerned, I'm a thirty year-old in a body over twice that age.

Quite a few years ago I had an older friend who's, sadly, now gone. He was old enough to be a Naval Academy classmate of Richard Byrd, the Antarctic explorer. He was a dear, dear man well into his nineties when I knew him. I used to marvel at his mental prowess. He was in pretty good physical condition too but had started fail a bit. For entertainment he did mathematical puzzles. For someone who has difficulty balancing his checkbook, you can imagine how impressed I was with this man who, in his nineties, did calculus for fun. I learned a lot from him. I think the principal lesson learned was the need to keep one's mind agile. He did it with calculus: I'm attempting to memorize an entire book of naughty limericks.

One of the sad things I've noticed is my friends aging. I haven't wanted to say anything but I can see wrinkles in a few. I, on the other hand, except for a few pounds, sagging bags under my eyes, scars on my bald head from where the dermatologist has burned off pre-cancerous lesions, the ache in my lower back and all those caramel-colored spots on my hands, don't show any age at all. My wife stays on my case all the time about hairy ears and the few fibers that poke out of my nose but I believe those are not new…she's just got pickier: maybe it's her age.

Somebody told me that ears keep growing as we get older. This is an interesting theory. I come from a family who are well-endowed in the auricular sense. I've studied this *ears keep growing theory* and get mixed information. Some very smart people seem to think they do, others don't. Being a little concerned that when I do get old I'll look even more like Dumbo, I've got my own theory. I think it's just gravity. I think those of us blessed with overlarge ears suffer, with time, what ladies with overlarge...well, you know...suffer. I think the ears just sort of sag and that makes them look overlarge. At least that's what I'm hoping.

The same theorists who espouse the overlarge ear theory comment on noses too. I have to be careful here because my adult leadership is sensitive about noses: see fibers above. I'm pretty sure the nose I've got is well established and does not intend to grow larger if ever I do get old. This is a good thing because I come from a family that's been known, in addition to oversized ears, to produce a prodigious proboscis or two. My nose has always been a source of pride to me. Back in the days when I was scouting for mates, the ladies would comment on my nose. Bill, your nose is beautiful. Things like that: but no more, no sir. The damn thing has developed these little pits and has turned various shades of red. Nose looks like a piece of raw sirloin. I'm going to get some therapy for that.

When I was a kid the black and white television came of age. I remember our first one: had great cowboy movies every day after school. The idea of a color television was so remote, I doubt many even considered it. Back then, plasma was something they never had enough of in the war movies. Today we have color, plasma televisions. Yeah, I know, it's a different kind of plasma but that's my point. We even have a new vocabulary. One of my chores as a kid was picking blackberries: today you punch out text-messages on them. A dear friend recently sent me a picture from a 1954 issue of a popular magazine showing a theorist's concept of a home computer in the future. Damn thing looked like the control room on a submarine: took up a whole wall. Look at where we are with computers today. Back when I was eating peanut butter sandwiches and watching cowboy movies on a black and white TV, I could not have imagined where we are technologically today. What would Flash Gordon think? Don't know Flash Gordon? Hmmm.

If I were aging…and I'm not…I think the automobile would be the thing most indicative of my advancing years. When I was a kid I was proud of my ability to identify every car on the road…and I could too. When I got older, tinkering with cars and racing became a passion. I was a pretty good mechanic and not too bad a driver. Today I cannot tell one car from the next. They all seem to look the same. Somebody asks me what I think of the newest models and I have to beg forgiveness. I do not understand the mechanics of any of them. I cannot even change the sparkplugs on the family station wagon. In fact, I can't even see the spark plugs. I don't even know if the damn thing has spark plugs. With today's engineering, maybe they've alleviated the humble spark plug. Now we're going to these hybrid things and I'll be even more confused. I knew when catalytic converters came along and you had to have an advanced degree in chemistry just to understand how the blinking exhaust system worked, we were in trouble.

My adult leadership says I'm becoming a curmudgeon. I think that means old grouch. I really don't think that's a product of age. I'm more inclined to believe it's a product of experience. During my many decades you meet a lot of people. A lot of them are people you'd rather not have met. Then somebody comes along who reminds you of one of those people whom you'd rather not have met and you long ago decided that you don't like people like that and it's hard to be friendly. That's what my sweetie calls grouchy. I'm not grouchy; I just don't like some kinds of people. To be sure, a person with less experience would not recognize so many personality types and would, therefore, be nicer to more people…at least until they've accumulated a little more data. I am meeting more and more dogs that I like and that certainly is not the sign of a curmudgeon.

Well, I'm a little stiff from sitting here at this computer for so long. And I have to take a whiz again…third time this morning. And what's his name is supposed to call me. What is his name? Just can't recollect. But I ain't old yet: a littler wiser perhaps; maybe a little weathered. I'm just not going to declare old for some time.

Resolutions of a Former Rag Sailor: *Back then it was fun*

Come on, you have to admit it…sailboats are pretty. For a short while, I lived in Rhode Island. Once, as my daughter and I sailed up Narragansett Bay, a big element of the New York Yacht Club came down, spinnakers flying. Those big blossomy sails were of every color and design imaginable. We were in a little mercury sailboat beating our way along and these guys were on both sides of us and in front. They were magnificent. You could retire comfortably on what some of those people paid for some of those sails. Wow!

Where I grew up, there wasn't a whole lot of sailing. There were a few sailboats but mostly folks seemed to prefer power. The Gulf of Mexico off the part of Florida where we lived is kinda shallow…and storms would pop up like whack-a-moles. I think people liked to have the option of full throttle and the bow towards shore when the boomies began…and not have 6 to 8 feet of keel hanging beneath them. But sailing always fascinated me.

Once, during my obnoxious years, I rigged a purloined bed sheet sail on my hot rod…a two-by-six plank with wheels. I persuaded my younger brother to be the test pilot while I worked as supervising engineer. Wind was no problem: the hot fields around us sucked air off the Gulf in great gulps. That sea breeze seemed to be ideal propulsion for our experimental rocket car. I didn't know a bowline from a granny-knot back then but I did know pirate ships. In the movies, pirate ships had these square sails that looked a lot like big bed sheets. The street where we lived was perfect: that street was a wind tunnel. I outfitted my younger sibling with an old leather football helmet, re-nailed the half-a-bushel basket seat so his feet could reach the axel to steer and raised the sail. I don't know why I didn't put that sail behind him. I could have. I just didn't think about it. It never even occurred to me that with the sail raised he couldn't see squat. Didn't think about brakes either. Worked out okay though. When he went off the embankment at the other end of the street, he kinda got caught up in the sail and his forward momentum was arrested. A little Merthiolate and some Band Aids and he was good as new.

My interest in sailing went into the doldrums when I discovered girls. When you're messing about with girls, you want to be handling them, not a whole bunch of sails and lines. I discovered the value of an old jon-boat and a putt-putt outboard. You could get into some wonderful skinny dipping places in that rig. Never once saw a sailboat back there in those rushes and reeds. I stayed on that tack for quite a while.

I entered active duty with Uncle Sam's Canoe Club in 1965. I reported for training at the Great Lakes Naval Station. Great Lakes, as it is called by all who know it, is perched on bluffs overlooking beautiful Lake Michigan. Once I overcame the fact that it was the middle of summer and I couldn't get warm and that you can have surf in fresh water, I couldn't wait to get out on Lake Michigan. When I learned the recreation department had sailboats, I thought I'd found nirvana. I got introduced to the Navy's fleet of Interlake Sailboats.

The little wooden 18-foot Interlakes were pretty as could be: the instructors responsible for them were not. I got assigned to a boatswain's mate who hated. Notice I didn't qualify that. You name it he hated it. And he hated students most of all. That was the snarliest son-of-a-whatever I have ever met: and I have met some. I pretty well knew my sailboat nomenclature so my instructor said seatrial. Not only was he snarly, he was a screamer. I did not realize, in the flower of my youth, that sailboats and screamers go hand in hand: I would meet many more. I passed my test but was deaf for a week.

I sailed the little Interlakers as much as I could. I rediscovered girls, which set me back some and the Marines decided to go ashore in

Vietnam which set me back even further. I had to focus on things other than play for a bit. My old instructor went on to be awarded big medals for driving boats in Vietnam: probably just yelled at the enemy.

In 1970 I reported for duty at the Naval Air Station, Corpus Christi, Texas. That's a pretty place. My boss, the base medical officer, was a rag sailor. I told him I had experience and he let me know my fitness report, in part, depended on how well I sailed. Being of the ensign persuasion in those days, lower than whale droppings, I said aye sir and where do I report. I crewed for him for 2 years: lots of blue water racing. He could have been the boson's cousin: the man had a set of lungs. I survived but he didn't, unfortunately. I've always suspected his untimely demise might have been at the hands of a former crewmember.

Well, time passed. I crewed for several others and discovered yelling was an art form among racing skippers. I got better at crewing and was less often the object of the epithets…to my great relief. I married a rag sailor. She wasn't a screamer but her father was. I sailed as much as I could with what little time I had. I avoided racing.

Some years passed. My rag sailor wife and I decided to go off on different tacks. And I found a new lady…who didn't know a jib from a jackstay.

When I suggested we should charter a sailboat for our honeymoon she said fine, as long as we tied up where she could plug in her hair dryer. My eyes were clouded by love. I was sure she would instantly become a world-class rag sailor. I never realized how many parts of a sailboat are called *whatzits*.

I have a friend, a former rag sailor, who has a powerboat named *No Strings*. I have seen several others so named. On either side of the name, he has those circles with the slash that everyone knows means no, superimposed and the silhouette of a sailboat. I now understand. I have given up the strings and the rags. There is real pleasure in aiming the bow towards a safe harbor, advancing the throttle, and going straight in: no screaming, no flapping, no booms cracking you on the noggin, no hour or so putting it all back together at the pier. I have resolved to be a rag sailor no more. I am now a bona fide *stinkpotter*, a powerboat sailor, and proud of it. I do enjoy watching the Friday night races off the local yacht club though. The sailboats are pretty and when those spinnakers blossom…magnificent. A little nostalgia sets in when I hear the sound of wind in the rigging and the flapping of the sails as they come about…then you hear the skippers screaming.

Quackers: *Life was just ducky*

Let me introduce you to Huey, Dewey, and
Louise. For years the three were inseparable. Huey
and Dewey were striking in their mallard finery,
iridescent green and blue predominant. Louise was
more subtle befitting her responsibilities to remain
camouflaged while upon the nest. Occasionally,
she would coyly reveal the little splash of blue
under her wing, in dramatic contrast to the rest of
her mottled brown feathering. Mallards, known for
sexual proclivities not discussed in polite
company, often are seen waddling in threesomes.
Huey, Dewey and Louise found this sort of
relationship comfortable. Cathy and Bill, in whose
yard, the three often slept, chattered, and
gamboled, figured out early on that the threesome
was platonic; or, as Cathy and Bill termed it,
incompetent.

We who live in our small town of Oxford,
Maryland joke about our ducks. A traffic jam in
Oxford is when you stop to let a momma duck and
her babies cross the road. Over by one of the
boatyards resides a gaggle of mixed breeds that we
call the Oxford irregulars. There is a white,
domestic goose who seems to be the provider of
the Y-chromosome to this motley bunch. His
progeny are spotted black and white, some with
brown and green, some with necks that look like

they belong on a stork, some just plain ugly. He's very proud of this crowd though and is seldom far from them...except when he's mooching over at Victor and Susan's fabulous ice cream emporium, The Highland Creamery. I think the early females of this mélange were probably mallards though it is no longer easy to spot any mallard-osity. Which was my point about mallards' bedroom choices.

By any measure Huey, Dewey and Louise had an idyllic existence together. When they felt like getting their webs wet, they'd paddle out to one of the small racing sloops anchored off *The Strand*, the street that parallels the Tred Avon River in Oxford and sun themselves on its small decks. Just to let the boat's owner know how much they appreciated his sharing the boat, they'd leave little calling cards. And then they'd fly to shore and waddle up to Cathy and Bill's for a snooze. Food was never a problem: up the street folks put out a little ducky banquet of shelled field corn. Not supposed to do that...the rats come out of the rip-rap and dine on the leftovers. But the threesome didn't mind sharing with the rats or the other birds that frequented the feast.

And then...the interloper arrived.

To hear Cathy and Bill talk about the interloper, you'd think he arrived smoking a cheroot and sporting a pair of pearl-handled .44's.

With a patch over one eye, he waddled on the
scene with his good eye on Louise. At first the
threesome was terrified of the interloper. On one
of the interloper's early visits, the two boys
panicked and midst flying feathers and gravelly
male duck talk, left poor Louise to her own
devices. Quacking and quaking, the terrified
Louise stood facing the evil interloper. Fortunately
Cathy was nearby and Louise took refuge behind
her. The interloper spit a couple of times, scratched
an indelicate itch and flew back behind the old,
closed restaurant where he had a poker game going
with some green herons. Huey, Dewey and Louise
gathered themselves and took a nap.

It's not uncommon to see female mallards
with two male escorts. As previously suggested,
these proclivities seem a little kinky but you never
know. Usually an observed trio is waddling along
munching on grass and bugs or paddling around in
the waters of the creek or river. What goes on in
the privacy of wherever they find privacy is
something they do not share. Occasionally, one of
the two males will get snippy and chase the other
away, but then disagreements are quickly forgotten
and the three will again move about together. If
she has a private moment with one and not the
other, it's not easy to tell. Ducklings look like
ducklings.

If Huey and Dewey had designs on Louise for more than companionship, Cathy and Bill never saw it. In these politically correct times, one cannot publically declaim on matters of sexual preference but, nevertheless, the thoughts will still invade our insensitive minds: we cannot duck it. What was the relationship between Huey and Dewey and if they did not notice how cute Louise was…why? Something to ponder. But Huey and Dewey were in for some rough times ahead. Louise disappeared.

Mallards are not the most refined sexual creatures. Occasionally, one will observe sexual calisthenics among a pair of mallards. The observer cannot but believe that the lady of the duo is not really enjoying the experience. To liken the activities to the interrogation method known as water-boarding is not a canard. She gets dunked repeatedly while Mr. Amorous flaps and squawks. It's not pretty. To even think of poor Louise experiencing this crude and insensitive ritual can only leave one saddened. But somewhere, somehow, she did.

Over there behind the old restaurant, a mother duck and her ducklings were observed. Sitting atop an old decorative piling, smoking a cheroot, iridescent green feathers sparkling in the sunlight, a male mallard watched the brood. The mother duck fussed with her babies, getting them ready for their first march to the water. The male finished his smoke, threw down the butt, scratched an indelicate itch and flew off into the sunset. Male mallards do not get involved in raising their young.

Without their common denominator, Huey and Dewey have parted ways. Louise is no longer the Louise they knew. She's worldly now. Huey and Dewey are just boys she knew when she was a maiden. Raising her babies was tough. It seems every critter higher on the food chain than a duck likes to eat duck babies: snakes, turtles, other birds, critters with four legs. Once she'd left the interloper's place behind the old restaurant, where the poker table still weathers in the summer sun, she didn't come back. She blended into the several duck families that live in Town Creek here in Oxford. The babies have grown their intermediate feathers and look a lot like their mom. Soon the males will get their iridescent green and the ladies their little flash of sparkling blue. Louise will be thinking of next season and maybe the interloper will come back.

Mallards are not as plentiful as they were just a few years ago. Foxes have come to Oxford in pursuit of the rabbits that have overrun the town. Every once in a while, foxes like a little duck, alfresco. Not long ago, someone spotted a fox with a large male mallard in its mouth. Maybe there was an eye patch too.

Over by the ice cream place, the white goose, his craw filled with the ends of ice cream cones, was seen looking at a cute little female mallard. She looked back. He honked. She didn't seem alarmed at the foreign language. He paddled closer. She thought, *he's almost as cute as the interloper.*

My Grandparents: *Did you know you can down a dragonfly with tobacco juice?*

Grandparenting has been on my mind a lot lately. It seems every time I look up there's another little critter running around our house: it's wonderful. It's still a new phenomenon to me though. I've discovered that new parents really don't want advice from their own parents: unsolicited advice engenders some horrific looks. I've had a few of those looks. Fine by me, I'll just play with the little wonders and tease them and get all those hugs and kisses and funky art work.

I was blessed with good grandparents. I don't think, however, two sets of people could have been more different than my respective grandparents. My paternal pair was of the ilk that believed children were to be seen and not heard: you know the type. They loved us and shared their love in many ways but they were kind of remote. My mother's parents though were totally opposite. They made us kids feel like we were important and visits to their farm was like a trip to Disneyland with adventures everywhere. They were strict and the rules were clear: violations got immediate and severe rebukes followed by reassurance and hugs…a wonderful way to raise children in my opinion. I loved both sets of grandparents but I think you can see which my favorites were.

My mother's father was a study in strength of character. He was not a big man but he had a big heart. I guess the adjective that best describes him is frugal. But that connotes someone who might not be generous and he was generous, often taking care of families that had been sharecroppers on his father's farm who had fallen on difficult times. I guess, perhaps, it's best to say he practiced economy. This applied to the farm and to his conversation, even to his affection. He would sit quietly listening to conversation, occasionally uttering *that's bull,* avoiding the second half of the aforementioned word, or nodding his head in agreement, depending on the position he took. It was hard to get him to talk about anything but his farm, it was even harder to get him to emote. He would smile or frown and that was about it. We kids would tease him by sneaking up on him and kissing him on the cheek. That would get us a *that's a lot of bull,* a response from him that was downright loquacious. And it would get us one of those rare smiles.

My maternal grandfather read everything. He subscribed to several farm magazines and would apply things he read to his farm. He often would consult with regional experts and his neighbors would come to him for advice. He was the first in his community to have a tractor, the first to have electricity and indoor plumbing. He practiced farming techniques that were unheard of in his time but are common practice today. I wish I had known these things when I was a kid. I would love to sit down with him as an adult and ask him about how he ran his farm. He was a wonderful grandfather.

When I think of a model grandparent though, it's my maternal grandmother, my Nanny that gets my vote. Compared to her husband, she was downright garrulous. She had an easy, hearty laugh and loved off-color jokes. She dipped snuff and chewed tobacco and was deadly with a stream of tobacco-juice, wiping out dragon flies perched on the flowers in front of her porch, as she sat in her rocking chair in the early evening. She was a big woman, very intelligent, who could converse with anyone and hold her own in conversions about religion, economics, politics, farming and just about anything else. She had an insatiable curiosity: she would quiz visitors in her home absorbing every little bit of new information. When television finally worked its way into rural North Florida, she became a news junkie. She would argue heatedly with the newscasters when she disagreed with their reports, often directing language at them that caused my mother to remind her that children were present. She would blush, apologize, and go right back to arguing with the face on the television screen.

My grandfather kept a few dairy cows. The milk and butter that came from these beautiful Jersey cows were consumed mostly by the family. He believed that if you treated the cows like ladies, they would be more productive: it was funny to hear him speaking endearments to a bunch of cud chomping cows. My grandmother hated cows. She hated cows so much, she wouldn't eat beef. It was her job to do the milking. All other aspects of cow husbandry were handled by my grandfather or us kids. Nanny milked the cows. Nanny cursed the cows. All of the nice things my grandfather said to his ladies were doubly offset by what my grandmother said to them. You see, cows have gas, lots of gas. And they exercise little in the way of politesse when the urge strikes. My grandmother would be sitting on her stool milking away when the cow would let one: the cow turned the air green, my grandmother turned the air blue. I have seen her haul off and slug a cow who was particularly prolific.

One of my grandmother's strictest rules applied to the farm cats. These cats, she warned, were not to be played with. They were for rodent control. This seemed to be fine with the cats who expressed their lack of domesticity with a swipe of their switchblades if a kid got too close. Regrettably, cats, house and farm, make other cats. Spaying was not an option; destroying the kittens was. To my grandmother destroying a litter of kittens was not a lot different than ringing a chicken's neck, something I saw her do many times. To this day I can remember my horror as I watched her destroy a litter of kittens. This side of her was all business: sentiment had no place.

This profane, tobacco chewing, kitty-killing woman could also be the gentlest, most loving person in the world. She had six grandsons. She loved every one of them. Maybe Nanny learned about boys from her own brothers: she had two, both older. She had had two daughters of her own. She knew that boys needed adventures and that they learned best from experience. She took time to teach us and trusted that we had judgment. She set boundaries that were seldom crossed: her response to infractions was swift and dramatic. When we captured live snakes and brought them home, she taught us how to care for them and explained why we should let them go. When we were little, we would sit on her lap as she rocked in that porch chair and sniped at dragonflies.

Some say that heaven is not some place in the outer galaxies but rather the memories one leaves on earth after they've departed. I kind of like that philosophy. If you subscribe to that theology, my grandparents are in paradise. I can only hope that those little wonders who provide me with all that crayon-drawn abstract art will someday sit down and remember their Grandpa

Dial with the same affection I remember my
Nanny: heaven!

The Gift of Grandchildren: *Nana rode a dinosaur*

My adult leadership and I spent last weekend with three of our eleven grandchildren, the parents of which were attending a wedding some distance from their home. The three, Miles, Riley, and Cooper are sweet kids. All our grandchildren are sweet kids. I ain't stupid: if they weren't do you think I'd admit it in writing? But that's not a problem because they all are...sweet that is.

I have a confession to make. I'm not all that fond of little kids. Well, that's not true...I'm very fond of them, I just don't get all worked up about them. I like to play with them for an hour or so and then go read a book. The adult leadership, on the other hand, gets worked up. Almost drooly. We're going to see the grandkids, let's go spend our next three months' income on them. Tell me, do you really think a one-year-old gives a flying whatever for those little butterflies on his onesie? Don't know what a onesie is huh? Neither did I. That's that one-piece rig with the snaps in the crotch to make it more efficient when you change the critter's britches. Back to the butterflies...really, I don't think a kid barely past his first anniversary cares for much more than being dry and where's the next meal coming from. And what can be done to interfere with older brothers' games. Well, before it was done we'd created a ten-foot tall pile of onesies trying to find the perfect little butterfly appliqué. The store lady implied my wife's behavior was normal. Scary! Anyway, I went happily along on the visit with an admonition from the adult leadership to behave myself.

I'll tell you something really scary: that's how bright little kids can be. And conniving. And crafty. Don't engage in mental gymnastics with a five year-old who's determined. You will lose. You can come up with your very best argument for why you should go for a walk after you've had your nap…me, not the kid… and the kid will rephrase the question a hundred times. *Grampa, how long will your nap be? Will you get ready for a walk before the nap so that when the nap is over we can go right away?* Don't fall for that one…doze off and you automatically lose control of how long your nap will be. Just about the time you lapse into high decibel snoring, you awaken with a start and two little guys are staring at you. The three year-old smiles and says, *Grampa, I like you.* That just isn't fair: conniving, crafty. They take after their grandmother. I had a good time on the walk. We chased butterflies and threw rocks and sticks into the Shenandoah River, about a hundred yards from their home. We lay in the grass and spotted pirate ships in the clouds and boats and trucks and when we were ready for home, they were bushed. And so was I.

SpongeBob SquarePants: that's a cartoon dude who's supposed to be a sea sponge but looks like he came in a package of six from off the shelf in the detergent aisle at Safeway. He lives on the bottom of the Pacific and flips hamburgers for a living...and regularly burns down the hamburger joint where he works. Duhh...he burns down a hamburger joint at the bottom of the Pacific. This program has won all kinds of awards. You ask me, there's something weird going on here. About half the time the character loses his square pants and runs around in his tidy whities. Kids love it though. They know all the characters and have memorized most of the episodes. You ask me, Wile E. Coyote was a heap more entertaining and was thought provoking as well: don't mess with that roadrunner. And when you grow up buy stock in that *Acme Company* Wile E. frequented.

One interesting thing about modern kids, they have interesting books. When I was a kid we were so poor, I learned to read with the Sears Roebuck Catalog and there wasn't that much light out there in the privy. I'm enthralled with the books kids have today. I remember a popup book about the Easter Bunny when I was little...belonged to a neighbor. Today kids have popup books about everything you can think of and the art is incredible. Dinosaurs and castles and history and everything else has been rendered in these magnificent books. And there is some serious engineering behind them too. To make a T-Rex pop up over and over and not be crunched is amazing. I think that popup Easter Bunny had an early demise.

I really enjoy reading to the little ingrates. I ham it up something awful and they giggle and ask me to read the same passage over and over. It's kind of neat...where else can you get an audience like that? Another neat thing is you can sort of tuck them under your arms while you read. That way they can point to things and ask questions. I'm very serious about my responsibilities in misinforming. They've got teachers and parents to straighten it out. Their grandmother did have a dinosaur saddle.

Things are so different today compared with when my own grown pair were babies. I've heard some folks complain about the new way of doing things and how we managed, and our adult kids managed, to survive in spite of being placed on our tummies in the crib. Well, I'm prepared to learn something new with regards to raising babies. Anything that can be done to keep them healthy and happy I'm all for. Few things are sadder than the death of an infant.

It's fascinating to watch the minds of children work. You really can tell what they're thinking...some of the time. Cooper, the littlest of the three, likes to take things out of boxes and put them back. He does this methodically. Maybe some gee-whiz, child psychologist can watch that behavior and predict which way he'll go as an adult. It is intriguing. My adult leadership, Cooper's grandmother, is methodical and hyper-organized. Are Cooper's activities some indication that he has inherited this trait from his grandmother? Who knows but it is intriguing.

My stepdaughter, the mother of the aforementioned ankle biters, is a great mom. She lets her boys be boys. They are rough and tumble and pee behind bushes and get muddier than a clay road in summer squall. They are all boys and that makes me happy. They are fascinated with trucks and heavy equipment and building things. And their mom understands this and encourages it. And I think it's wonderful. There will be plenty of time later on for refinement. Right now they like to swing on ropes and catch bugs and build tree houses and be boys. Hoorah!

Little Cooper had a bad night the night we were there. Little guy had a cold and just couldn't sleep. We couldn't do anything to make him feel better it seemed. He had his medicine and didn't have a fever, he just coughed and coughed and cried. Finally, in the wee hours of the morning, I nestled him next to me and just stroked his shoulders. He settled down and his little fingers gently rubbed the hair on my arm. God, thank you for the gift of children.

Well, curmudgeon that I am, I have to make it clear that I'm not influenced by their behavior. I'm not affected at all when they lean up against me on the couch, pacifier in the mouth, and cuddle. Doesn't affect me. And when they look up and the clouds and say, Grampa, that looks like the dinosaur Nana used to ride. Yep, doesn't affect me. In all we have eleven grandchildren. They are as far away as Minnesota and Atlanta and one lives in heaven. We are blessed to have sweet Luke and Bryan who live just twenty miles from us. I cherish them all. And I learn from them. I marvel at them. When my own were little, I was so busy trying to get on with life, I missed a lot of things. That's the blessing of grandchildren. You can take time to see them become.

The Quality of Good Wood: ...*and that might not mean what it sounds like*

Note: We haven't seen Smiling Bob in a while but I'll bet most remember him. He was selling what used to be called snake oil. Obviously, word chosen carefully, what he was selling didn't do what he wanted you to believe it did. The ads were hilarious...that is, if you didn't believe him. Enjoy this bit of humor.

Ladies, excuse us for a minute: we need a little guy-talk here. Alright, fess-up: did you buy that stuff, you know, that enlarges your, uh, well, you know? It may not be you but somebody's buying it. Seems like all I see on the tube are advertisements for natural male enhancement pills. If people weren't buying it, they wouldn't keep advertising it, right? Did you buy some? Go ahead, admit it: we won't snicker. Well, maybe a little.

I have one of those little satellite dish systems. I like it a lot; couldn't count on the cable, every time it rained the thing shut down. My only complaint is Bob. Have you seen this turkey? Bob, it seems, had certain shortcomings. Then he discovered this magic potion that enhanced his, uh, marital situation. Now he walks around with this grin that looks like God gave him an extra ration of teeth. And he has this little mousey spouse who apparently is quite pleased with Bob's new gear. Pity that poor wife, if you believe that advertisement, she could get hurt.

If you haven't seen these ads, you need to. No, I don't mean you need to buy the product; you just need to see the ads. In one they say Bob has discovered the value of good wood. It shows a bunch of guys standing around in what appears to be a home improvement place, all of them, except smiling Bob, looking sort of down-in-the mouth. This store-guy is holding up a piece of mahogany and going on about the quality of wood. Our boy Bob isn't all droopy, no sir, the ad says he has learned the value of good wood and the importance of the right tools. Nothing is ever said about the product they're selling…just a not-so-subtle implication. If all those long-in-the-face guys buy this potion, it is implied, they can appreciate good wood too. We ain't talking cabinet making here guys if you're having trouble following me.

I looked this up this magic pill on the Internet. It's made out a bunch of herbs with African sounding names. I sort of expected dried bat wing and maybe some powdered rhino horn…nope, herbs. I wouldn't get near that stuff. I'd be afraid that smile of Bob's could be a side effect.

I commiserated with my wife about these ads. I told her Bob was starting to get to me…that toothy smile. I told her I was also tired of the half-dozen emails I get every day asking if I didn't think I needed to improve my situation. That combined with our boy Grinning-Bob and his wood thing, a fellow could get concerned, maybe wonder. My wife assured me all was well but she didn't offer a lot of sympathy. Men, she said, are just now getting what women have dealt with forever. She reminded me of all the potions hawked on the tube to treat PMS and other female maladies. She said her emails are full of ads for breast enhancements. I know when to hush.

The interesting thing about the enhancement potions is that they don't work. Knowing I was opening myself up to a barrage of ads touting enhancement products, I looked up their ingredients and actions on the Internet…carefully avoiding any that looked like ads. I read several articles written by urologists: all said there is no physiological basis for the claims made by the makers of male enhancement drugs. Apparently, what you got issued is what you're stuck with. So how do they get away with so much advertising? The small print says that these potions are in the same category as food supplements and vitamins: they are not intended to cure anything. Now I understand why the ads don't come right out and say what they're saying: that explains all the implications. What is male enhancement anyway? The ads never really say…just the wood stuff and all the tool allusions. I'm still curious though. To pay for all those ads, somebody's out there buying. Nobody I know confesses however.

I guess this concern for our manliness is sort of a universal problem. That's why products like Viagra seem to be doing so well…I think there are now two or three Viagra clones on the market. And talk about advertising allusions, one cautions that a person should get immediate help if the expected physiological reaction lasts for greater than four-hours. Man, I'll bet guys lined up at their doctors' offices after they heard about that possibility.

I saw a National Geographic program a while back that discussed the problem of rhinoceros poaching. The poachers only want the rhinos' horns: it's ground up and dispensed in certain Asian countries as a male enhancement potion…a practice that goes back to the beginning of recorded time apparently. Don't you wonder who the heck thunk that one up? I think maybe there was a little of that advertising hocus-pocus going on way back there in the mighty jungle. Visiting traders were probably told the rhinoceros was noted for its sustainability and, well, look at his size. Take a little of the ground-up rhino horn and stir it into your green tea and look out geisha girl: ever since the poor rhino has been stalked for his snout. And rhino horn peddlers have been laughing in their loin-clothes.

Remember when you were a kid, your big brother or maybe the kid across the street told you about Spanish fly? You remember! Your hormones were totally out of control, the device in your wallet was untested, and, as far as you could tell, nobody was interested in helping you prove or disprove your ability to use it. And your pal said all you needed was a little Spanish fly and a willing partner. When you finally got him to admit it, he told you he hadn't actually had any experience with Spanish fly but he'd heard about somebody who had. And no, he didn't really know where you could get any. I guess we start worrying about enhancements at an early age. (Spanish fly it turns out exists and is very poisonous…don't try and find some after all these years. If you haven't tried the thing in your wallet by now, talk to your doctor about some of those pills. By the way, I'm told those things in your wallet tend to rot, so if it's been there for a while, don't trust it.)

Seems to me we're probably going to have to endure ads for some form of male enhancement for a long time to come. As long as men are duped by those silly ads and go out and buy the products, those of us who have a little confidence are going to keep wearing out the mute button on the clicker. If folks are silly enough to believe some ad that uses allusions to the quality of wood and the right tools to convince us we are several inches short of a perfect life, I'm sad. But I guess they are: the barrage continues. I'm still waiting for a call from some bud who says he had to go out buy larger skivvies as a result of swallowing some African sounding herbs. Wood indeed!

Modesty Revealed: *When it revealed that I have no modesty*

I've read, or been enjoined to read, all the books on the astronomical origins of the respective gender. I'm prepared to accept that men are Martians. Heaven knows I've been around a few that certainly weren't from this planet. Concomitantly, I'll just have to accept that Venusian thing. Frankly, I don't have a clue where women come from...or came from...so it just might be Venus. I do know that, in most cases, they speak some language that I don't comprehend. Take modesty for example.

The other day we were cruising on the Choptank River near Cambridge, Maryland. The day was pretty, the dog was sleeping on the after deck and I was driving. My adult leadership was the only other soul on board and she was sitting in the sun back aft. It was the middle of the week so boat traffic on the river was almost nonexistent. My better half asked if I thought it would be safe to take off her top and do a little tanning. Well, that gave me a little salacious shiver; after all she's not bad for the accumulation of all those years. I quickly acknowledged my support for the idea. I was fairly certain the beautiful day was about to get prettier. What I didn't understand, due to the aforementioned incompatibility of language, was that taking off her top simply meant that. The underlying undergarment, built of material left over from the construction of flak jackets for Marines and engineered like a construction derrick, was to remain in place. I was asked to advise when another boat approached within ten miles so that the previously removed shirt could quickly be pulled up so as not to reveal the eighth of a square inch of flesh exposed.

When I began my naval career, I was assigned to a small, naval reserve, destroyer escort based in Pensacola, Florida. My first active duty consisted of a two week cruise down into the Caribbean. Like most males of my generation, I'd endured open showers in the gym and the occasional all-male skinny dipping adventure in a swimming hole, so modesty was not something I'd thought much about. There was one head, a bathroom, for the enlisted crew on the USS TWEEDY. It consisted of twelve stainless steel toilets, six on each side. The toilets were so close, you literally rubbed cheeks with the persons on the adjacent pot. One learned to time one's toilet. The point is that men don't worry too much about modesty. That head was designed by a man and had been in service, at that point in time, for over twenty years. My timing of toilet was more olfactory than modesty related.

I lived in Germany for three years. My *then wife* had no compunctions about modesty. Soon after arriving in Germany we stayed in a hotel in Munich that had a co-ed sauna. Outside the sauna was a sign with the familiar red circle and slash with what appeared to be a pair of boxer shorts contained within: nude sauna. *Then wife* stripped faster than a boy with a bee up his britches and disappeared into the mists. I was not as hasty. I stood there pondering the possibilities when a delightfully provided young woman came out of the sauna and stood under the nearby shower. It only took but a few seconds for me to go sans pantaloons and join my frau. That was just the first exposure. I learned that Germans, as a group, eschew modesty. My *then wife* loved it.

My *now wife*, my beloved adult leadership, spends a lot of time in the garden, where she performs horticultural miracles. Her standard gardening costume consists of attractive…and modest...shorts and sleeveless shirts. In the evening she joins me for television or reading in her nightgown. Her standard nightgown goes from her neck to her toes. In the summer it's light cotton; fall and winter, warm flannel: neck to her toes. Considerably more flesh is hidden than when in the standard gardening costume. When she descends the stairs in her nightgown, the shades are drawn, the lights dimmed, the mirrors covered, the dog wears blinders and I'm not allowed to look...and she's covered neck to toes. Now somebody explain that to me.

I happened to mention the aforementioned modesty phenomenon to a friend of my wife's, a person of the feminine persuasion. When I asked her why a full length nightgown brought on more modesty than the usual gardening attire, she looked at me like I was from another planet. I realized very quickly that I was in great danger of being told to go back to Roswell with others from my origin.

So there you have it. Maybe men are from another planet and we just don't have the capacity to understand the Venusian brain. Maybe we Martians need to just accept that we cannot expect to comprehend the variances and vagaries of our companion gender. For me the modesty thing is okay. Some of those Venusians aren't the least bit modest.

Enough Already: *That Team in Buffalo Needs a Name Change*

Note: A little dated but I'm still incensed.

I'm tired of my dignity being trashed. Hush, I do have dignity. I'm serious. Bills everywhere suffer from an insult and we're tired of it. I've talked to hundreds of Bills and we all agree: sports teams should not be named after us Bills. Of course I'm referring to the Buffalo Bills and if you are in team management, look out. Us Bills are going to rise up. You better be looking for another name.

This cavalier use of mascots and names has plagued the sports industry for years. It is thoughtless for the owners and operators of these teams to just choose some moniker and go on as though no one cares. The Native Americans were the first to point this out and now I think it's time for others similarly impacted to sound off.

There's danger in animal mascots too. Animals have dignity. I'm amazed that the People for the Ethical Treatment of Animals (PETA) haven't made more noise about this. Consider the poor terrapin. The University of Maryland exploits this slow creature with total disregard for the dignity of the terrapin. Turtles are helpless

290

creatures. When intelligence was issued, I think the turtle missed out because it took so long for it to get to the table. How many times have you dodged a turtle in the middle of the road? Or, maybe, stopped and assisted the poor creature out of the traffic lanes? This is not an animal you'll ever see on the Noble Prize list. To exploit the turtle in the shameless way Maryland does is certainly unethical: PETA listen up.

Everybody knows that sports teams are sweaty, stinky, uncouth, collections of over-developed roughnecks. They scratch and spit and use awful language. To have one's name associated with people of this ilk is just, well, embarrassing. Sure, it takes a lot of courage to go out there and fight for a team, smashing and banging and running up and down a field. But do you really want to have you name associated with this? If there were teams called the Cincinnati Roberts or the Miami Michaels you'd hear some folks protesting. That's what has caused us Bills to rise up.

And no mythical creatures either. Gnomes are out: these beings are believed to be real to some folks and to use them in this highly derogatory way would be just…ignominious. Gnomes really have been treated shabbily. There's a current ad on television where a poor gnome gets beat up and run over and folks think it's funny.

There are caves full of gnomes in Finland incensed about this. And that little red hat: gnomes, I'm told, prefer something that resembles an old top-hat. So if the Greensboro Gnomes cricket team asks you for a donation don't do it. Respect the gnome. No trolls or unicorns either.

How many teams do you know that use the cougar as a team name and mascot? See, here's an animal that's endangered. Now you would think that the strength and beauty of this great cat would make it the ideal candidate for a team's name. Not so. If you, say, are a fan of the Baltimore Blue Bonnets curling team and you happen to see a cougar crossing the road after your wonderful Blue Bonnets have been trounced by the Cougars, you might just gun the engine and smash that cat even though it's on the endangered list. You can't have that sort of thing so animals on the endangered lists can't be used.

When I was but a pup, my father was a student at the newly founded Florida State University. My earliest memories are of the Seminoles, the symbol of FSU athletics. Now here's an interesting study. The Chairman of the Seminole Tribe of Florida says he thinks it's a great idea for FSU to use the Seminole as a symbol. I always thought it honored the Seminoles to use them thusly. But even with the tribe's acceptance, the FSU Seminoles are in trouble. The

National Collegiate Athletic Association, the NCAA, has dictated that no team using Native Americans as symbols will be allowed to play in NCAA sponsored events. So there you are. The NCAA certainly knows best wouldn't you say? The jury is still out but right now FSU is telling the NCAA to stuff it.

I think it's important in this age of sensitivities that we consider these things. Shoot, I think we should have a National Naming Council. Their approval would be required before anything was named. They would ensure there were no abuses. Consider breakfast cereals: you wouldn't want that Quaker dude on your oatmeal box if you knew it was going to offend some pagan would you? That's what I mean. I think it was thoughtless of them to put that guy there when somewhere some person is heartbroken all through breakfast, all because of that image. The Naming Council would be composed of really sensitive people who would stop this.

The Council would have the authority to go out and find areas where sensitivities were being trounced by improper names. Certainly they would put a stop to the Pontiac. And towns too like Indianapolis. Back in Florida every river would have to be renamed. And it's high time. State names would have to go: Massachusetts and Delaware look out. And anything named after somebody who's dead: didn't get their permission. You have to admit that, in the name of politesse, this is the right thing to do.

Back to the Bills: I know team management is going to see my point here. I'm going to try and think of some good names they can use. I think, maybe, vegetable names would be okay. I think the Buffalo Bell Peppers has a ring to it. No, I know some people named Pepper: they wouldn't be pleased. Maybe the Buffalo Carrots. I can see somebody in a carrot suit dancing on the sidelines. The use of vegetable names really opens a lot of opportunities. The Washington Fighting Asparagus: that'd work. How about the Pittsburgh Pears?

There was a time when we Americans were tough. Our parents suffered through world wars and economic depressions and other such toughening experiences as these. Fortunately, we no longer have to be tough and we can explore our sensitivities. Exploiting someone's name or title is just not something appropriate for our times. Be glad we've arrived at this high state of civilization.

I think it's right and proper for those of you out there who revel in our improved societal mores to approach persons abusing names or symbols. Tell them to stop it. For example, do you know someone who drives a Plymouth? That's where those darned Pilgrims landed: religious connotations. Just suggest they put a little duct-tape over the name of their car: they'll understand. Me: I'm going to protest the use of the term *bill* for dunning notices. I think they should be termed *dunning notices*. Rats, I know someone named Dunning.

Finis or not *Finis*, that is the Question... .

My apologies to Mister Shakespeare.

In the forward to this tome I mentioned that I had written over 200 columns in my column writing days. For this effort, I picked my very favorite. However, my adult leadership is on my case again to publish a few more. I might.

This has been fun. The Kindle version of this book, both in e-book and paperback, has been very well received. Our parish priest has assured me that I'm number one on the hospital bed circuit. When doing his pastor bit, he reads my columns to the patients. I hope that doesn't extend their stay. Seriously, that is quite a compliment. I've been told it makes a great "bathroom book." When visiting the necessary, one might bide their time reading a few of the columns. Okay as long as they don't mistake it for the toilet paper.

I've been asked a few times to talk to groups regarding this book and my other, *Memoir of an Adventurous Life: Vietnam Before and After* (highly recommended) and the challenges of self-publishing. I've enjoyed talking with other writers and authors and highly recommend the process. It has been a great learning experience for me.

Stay tuned: there may be another *Just Saying*. *Finis* for now.

90980754R00171

Made in the USA
San Bernardino, CA
23 October 2018